HOW TO TALK TO ANYONE WITH EASE

9 CRUCIAL SKILLS TO CONNECT WITH PEOPLE,
MASTER SMALL TALK, AND HAVE BETTER
CONVERSATIONS ANYTIME

CHASE HILL

CONTENTS

YOUR FREE SAY NO CHECKLIST

DON'T LET THE PEOPLE PLEASING TRAP YOU AGAIN...

I'd like to give you a gift as a way of saying thanks for your purchase!

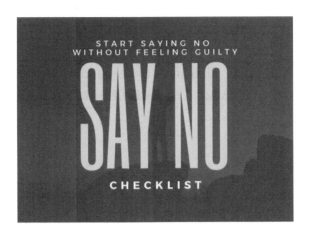

This checklist includes:

- 8 steps to start saying no
- 12 must-dos to stop feeling guilty

- 9 healthy ways to say no

The last thing we want is for your mood to be ruined because you weren't prepared.

To receive your Say No Checklist, visit the link:

www.chasehillbooks.com

Prefer a quick access? Scan the QR code below:

If you have any difficulty downloading the checklist, contact me at **chase@chasehillbooks.com,** and I'll send you a copy as soon as possible.

INTRODUCTION

You are at a party and stand with three or four other people. Your mouth won't let you speak. Your hands won't stop shaking, and no matter how hard you try to keep up with the conversation, you are always behind. You laugh at the wrong moments, and all of this makes you feel like everyone is laughing at you. The only thing you can do is leave!

How many times have you heard that humans are social beings? Did it start when you were at college or university? Or perhaps the concept pops up in TED talks or a podcast you heard recently. YouTube is flooded with videos with tips to communicate with confidence! And don't get me started on social media and the constant reminders of our need to socialize! Don't they all make it seem so easy?!

This encouragement, even pressure to be social, isn't anything new. It was Aristotle who wrote, "Man is by nature a social animal." But what did he really mean by this? His words probably implied that society was better off being civilized, which still stands true today. However, there is a massive difference between being civilized and being social.

Neuroscientists will agree on three things. First, our brains are wired to connect; second, humans are incredibly complex; and third, the ability to be social is a crucial element of our lives.

Regardless of your background and where you are in your life today, there will be a need to socialize and communicate, whether that's with your partner, your professor, or your colleagues.

Social behavior is a two-way process. Take empathy as an example. Throughout history, scientists have attempted to better understand social behavior by looking at an individual. But empathy is just one emotion that requires an empathizer and the person they are showing empathy toward. For successful interactions, there has to be empathy from both sides, or else only one person is capable of fully understanding.

With social interactions, we can learn more about ourselves and the world we live in. On an individual level, social behavior influences everything from what we wear to how we eat and how we talk to others.

On a grander scale, our interactions teach others about culture and the norms of life. Taking a child to a restaurant teaches them how to eat correctly and how to order food politely. Imagine walking into a restaurant with everyone chewing with their mouth open! All of these tiny details that make such a significant difference are learned through our social interactions.

The question may be, are our social interactions derived from nature or nurture? Studies on twins have shown that nature significantly impacts our social interactions. Twins, Elyse Schein and Paula Bernstein, were separated at birth and reunited 35 years later. Aside from looking the same, the twin adults had the same facial expressions and hand gestures.

Yet, when an American moves to a European country and spends enough time there, they will go back to visit the States and find themselves giving everyone two kisses rather than a handshake or a hug. So, nurture and our environment also determine social behavior.

In extreme cases, complete isolation from society has proven the importance of our interactions.

Isabelle was a 6-year-old girl who was found over half a century ago. She and her mother lived alone in a dark room in the family home. Her mother was mute and the two only communicated with a few simple gestures.

When she was found, Isabelle's behavior was similar to that of a wild animal, and in some situations, she was more like a child of six months old. Isabelle required years of intense training and support to be able to communicate at the same level as a child of her age (Davis, 1947).

Fortunately, you haven't reached the stage of extreme isolation, but there is still a severe problem when it comes to your social interactions.

"Just so hollow and ineffectual, for the most part, is our ordinary conversation. Surface meets surface. When our life ceases to be inward and private, conversation degenerates into mere gossip."

— HENRY DAVID THOREAU

Social interactions for you may feel like what Thoreau described, shallow and meaningless conversations with no true connection. For some, their lack of communication skills, whether that's speaking, listening, or body language, makes talking to people frustratingly impossible. You get spoken over, interrupted, or simply ignored.

At first, you might feel that these problems with communication don't have that much of an impact on your life. That is until you notice how shy you are becoming; you turn down invitations because it's easy to avoid social occasions. Before you know it, even the thought of social interactions creates so much anxiety that you feel frozen.

The fear starts playing over and over in your head, and you start telling yourself that you are stupid. And now, your confidence and self-esteem are damaged.

To top it all off, you are actually highly intelligent, have great ideas, and are skilled at problem-solving and decision-making—all of which are also essential life skills. But in this place of self-doubt, you can't get your opinions across. So, the consequences continue when a project goes badly at work, or a major decision is made at home, and you can't express your concerns.

What may at first appear to be a lack of communication skills can lead to other people making important decisions and, basically, leading your life for you.

What can be learned can be unlearned. Your brain has created connections that constantly tell you that you can't communicate well or socialize. Still, you can rewire these thoughts and learn how to improve your communication, be more assertive, and understand those all-important social cues.

By understanding how the brain works and how the body reacts during anxiety, you will be able to manage your thoughts and emotions. From there, you are going to learn what effective communication looks like and how to become confident and assertive in your interactions. Breaking your communication barriers will enable you to have deep, meaningful conversations with anyone you want to without feeling awkward or insignificant.

I have had my fair share of social interaction failures. Some, I can laugh at. With a love for traveling, I have experienced firsthand what it is like not being able to communicate and the confusion this creates. Other experiences had long-lasting impacts on my life. Being shy and somewhat passive, I let other people take advantage of my lack of skills, and this made me miserable.

Over a decade ago, I made a drastic change in my career and began researching psychology, assertiveness, boundaries, and healthy communication skills. My fascination with the human mind led me to become a life coach specializing in personal growth, stress management, and social interactions.

After the amazing feedback from my #1 bestseller, *How to Stop Overthinking*, I knew I could help more people by sharing both my personal experiences and knowledge.

What you are about to learn has been proven to work, not only by myself but also by hundreds of clients who are now leading a more fulfilling life, reaching their goals, and enjoying deeper relationships. Everybody had their challenges, but with the right guidance, they overcame them, and you will too.

Regardless of where you are in life, studying or working, employing others or healing wounds in relationships, or raising a family, improving your communication skills will prove to be invaluable on all levels and imperative for your happiness. Prior to jumping into an arsenal of techniques and strategies, it is necessary to take a closer look at the role of communication within society.

CHAPTER ONE: THE SOCIAL PILLAR YOU CAN'T DO WITHOUT

"The single biggest problem in communication is the illusion that it has taken place."

— GEORGE BERNARD SHAW

Understanding socialization as a series of stages finalized by a repeated cycle is helpful. Primary socialization begins at birth and is the foundation of our social communication. Everybody involved in a child's life plays a role in developing their personality and the first of their social skills, such as eye contact, listening, and learning how to talk.

As the child grows up, there are more influences both on their personality and social behavior. I'm not anti-technology in any way, but the misuse of the internet can encourage teens to break away from the ethics and morals their parents instilled.

During the secondary stage of socialization, people start to move away from their family's influences and discover their own values. A lot of this takes place in educational settings and with maturity. Older teens break away from peer pressure and represent their own ideologies in their groups.

The stage of practicing social skills and discovering what works and what doesn't is known as developmental socialization. We strengthen the skills that work and abandon those that don't. This is followed by anticipatory socialization, and our definite style of communication is formed, and people understand how relationships are built.

Throughout life, we may experience various resocializations, a process where we discard the usual communication style and habits in favor of new ones that are needed at the time. It sounds exhausting, but it's a good thing. Much like that, what can be learned can be unlearned; this continuous cycle of change means that we are all able to change our communication style, social skills and, essentially, our personalities.

So how does communication fit in?

The Social Pillar You Can't Do Without

Our brains' social capacity evolved. Humans haven't always been at the top of the food chain. Think back to early humankind when humans were up against larger and stronger predators. One man versus a tiger and the tiger has the upper hand. A group of men versus one tiger and man has a much greater chance of survival. Man quickly learned the importance of cooperation and communication to create a community.

It's the social evolution and our need to communicate to create communities that has pushed us forward as humans. Without such a strong desire to communicate, we may not have some of our most favored technologies of today.

Ever since the invention of the printing press, humans have strived to invent new ways to communicate. When I first left home to travel, I was excited that I would be able to email friends and family. Today, we can make video calls to anyone in the world for free.

Even then, without communication skills, these new technologies aren't going to be very fruitful.

The Importance of Communication Skills in Our Life

Recently, scrolling through social media to kill a few minutes, I spotted a video of a toddler sitting on his mom's lap. The title was "Look what happens when he hears his mom's voice for the first time." A doctor was fitting a hearing aid, and you could see that it was uncomfortable and a little awkward for the boy.

There is no way to describe the look on this toddler's face when he heard his mom's voice for the first time. It was pure delight and instant comfort and just one example of why communication is essential for all of us.

It's how we develop our relationships, ease conflicts, and understand more about ourselves and other people. It's how we exchange information, learn, and grow as a person.

If you think your success is dependent on your intelligence, you might be surprised to discover that it's quite the opposite. Approximately 85 percent of success is attributed to the ability to communicate well. The remaining 15 percent is down to your work skills (The Scientific World, 2020).

Strong communication skills improve all relationships—professional and personal—because people are able to convey their ideas, perspectives, and values. We need to appreciate that we live in a very diverse world, and being able to communicate effectively allows us to appreciate differences in opinions. How many of the world's problems could be resolved by accepting our differences?

The communication skills that we develop are what we need to be able to start accessing and improving our social skills. When you start a puzzle, you always go for the corners and the edges first. Once you have this structure, you can start completing the inside, and in this case, our social skills.

Social Skills Aside from Communication

We learn different social skills at different stages of our lives. For example, as children, we learn how to take turns, share, and follow directions. As teens, we develop patience, empathy, and respect for other people's boundaries.

By adulthood, it's normally the time for us to master these skills so that we can regulate our emotions, solve problems and conflicts, and develop our relationships in a variety of circumstances.

Our social skills and interactions are imperative, not only because our brain needs them. Right now, you may feel like your social interactions are the cause of your stress but being around people reduces the stress hormone cortisol. High levels of stress can lead to health problems such as heart disease. Studies have even shown that people with weaker social networks die younger (Berkman & Syme, 1979).

The brain works better when we are not alone. The backward and forward of a two-way conversation are easier for the brain to process than it is for a conversation with yourself.

What's more, those social interactions with people who drive us crazy actually help us to grow. These people who we don't always agree with expand our range of emotions. Feeling frustrated expands our abilities to feel good too.

Communication is only a part of our social skills. Let's take a look at how other social skills are vital for a successful and happy life.

Communication is only effective if the other party is actively listening, something that so many people neglect. They might be in the habit of making assumptions, guess what the next person is going to say. So instead of letting the other person finish, they interrupt.

When people actively listen, they are in a better position to give and receive feedback. Listening to the advice of superiors enables professional growth. Being able to provide your team members with feedback in the right way leads to successful results. Feedback isn't limited to the workplace. Sometimes, our friends, family, and even our children need direction in a kind and constructive way.

Every day we are faced with problems to solve and decisions to make. People need to be able to talk about problems and listen to different perspectives in order to make the right decisions. Having strong problem-solving skills puts people in a better position to take initiative.

In a world that often seems to be spiraling out of control, it seems that kindness and tolerance are somewhat lacking. Empathy or the "psychological superglue" is what connects people, creates prosocial behavior, and reduces aggression and bullying, racism, and judgment. Psychologists and neurologists pay a lot of attention to what is often considered the most important value in society.

Social skills don't stop at what we say and what we hear. Our nonverbal social cues give away the message we are trying to get across. Imagine giving a presentation on a new product, but your hands are shaking, and your eyes are darting all over the place. Your nerves could be interpreted as a lack of confidence in your own presentation.

On the other hand, if you are in an interview and sit up straight, you aren't fidgeting, and you are smiling and making eye contact, your body language communicates the same positive message that your resume states.

Studies produce different numbers, but as much as 90 percent of our communication is conveyed through body language (Thompson, 2011). Things like our posture, facial expressions, and gestures let others see more of our true feelings and problems, those that are often not conveyed with words.

When we look at the importance of all these social skills, we get to see the bigger picture. Accurately understanding body language and social cues, along with listening, is what leads to deep and meaningful communication. When we see the bigger picture, we are able to deliver a response that is appropriate, both in terms of words and emotions.

Considering the sheer importance of communication and social skills, we are now faced with two problems. The first goes back to the wise words of George Bernard Shaw. So many times, we make the assumption that effective communication has taken place but, in reality, the message isn't delivered effectively or interpreted accurately.

Let's take a moment to explore the extent of this problem. You tell your partner that you want steak for dinner, but they weren't listening properly and ordered Chinese instead. Thinking they were doing something nice, they ordered your favorite dish, but the waiter wrote it down wrong. Getting your takeaway delivery for a nice surprise, you are now angry because your partner "never" listens, and the argument begins.

The second problem is that we aren't born with natural social skills despite being a social species. By definition, it's a skill that we develop through social interactions, and though this begins as soon as we are born, it takes an awfully long time to master social skills.

The irony is that our communication and social skills training focuses on two components that account for the least amount of communication. Aside from body language, we have reading, writing, speaking, and listening.

For most, speech and language develop naturally with some linguistic education throughout school. This is 30 percent of communication.

Reading and writing are taught by parents, teachers, or a combination. Here, we have 16 percent and 9 percent, respectively.

It gets better! The average person can speak 125 to 175 words per minute, yet we are capable of listening to 450 words per minute (Steiger, 2019). Listening accounts for 45 percent of communication, so it's ironic that this skill is rarely taught.

And this is just one of the reasons why communication fails.

Why Communication Doesn't Go the Way We Had Hoped

It's easy to blame the listener for breakdowns in communication, but it's a two-way street! Some people genuinely struggle to pay attention, and their mind wanders rather than actively listen. At the same time, it could be the delivery of the message that impacts the listener.

There is such a thing as pseudo-listening, a type of non-listening. This occurs when people have too much on their minds, they are trying to multitask, or someone listens just because they don't want to cause offense, but really, the message isn't going in.

Pseudo listeners may feel they already have knowledge on the subject, so they don't make the effort to actively listen. Others fall into this trap because they are too busy finding flaws or mistakes to prove the speaker wrong.

Word choice and grammatical structures influence the interpretation of a message. Errors in the vocabulary we use or how we phrase our sentences may confuse the listener. Sometimes, people choose language that is more complex than it really needs to be, and the listener switches off. They may even become bored.

There will be times when communication doesn't go as planned because someone's ego gets in the way. People are so determined to be right that logic, reason, and the ability to compromise go out the window. This determination to be right stops us from listening and showing empathy.

I confess; if there is one thing that stops me from being able to listen, it is a lack of manners. When people try to get their point across in an aggressive or disrespectful way, it becomes very difficult to focus on what is being said. How it is being said is distracting! A lack of respect leads people to withdraw from the situation, even social events.

There are circumstances for communication breakdowns aside from how the message is delivered and interpreted. Our day-to-day lives are filled with diversity. We interact with people from diverse cultures and religions, different ages and genders, and a wide range of different experiences.

This means that not everyone is going to think the same way that we do. Even when we put ego to one side, sometimes, it's not about being right. It's just that beliefs and opinions are so different that people struggle to communicate.

Diversity means an equally wide range of different personalities. Personalities do clash because it's unrealistic to think that everyone will get on with everyone else. Communication with somebody who has a personality disorder becomes even more complex!

Without honesty and trust, communication will never be completely meaningful. Naturally, you can't trust someone who blatantly lies to you, but there is also the problem of people pleasing and even shyness. If someone only tells you what you want to hear, is that really genuine communication?

Finally, let's take a brief look at the characteristics that create communication barriers:

• Blaming: One person is always at fault while the other is the victim.

• Passive aggression: Giving people the silent treatment, denial, and distortion.

• Hopelessness: You have tried to communicate, but nothing works, so it makes sense to give up.

• Helping: Someone feels such a need to help and offer advice that they don't actually take the time to listen.

• Counterattack: Often seen at the beginning of an argument, a person doesn't like what they hear and respond with criticism or by becoming defensive.

• Sarcasm: The tone of voice doesn't match what the person may want to say; often, an attempt at humor comes across as hostility.

- Emotional blocks: When people aren't able to recognize emotions or handle them correctly. Words and body language can be fueled by emotion.

- Charisma: The charm of a person can cloud the message, but a lack of charisma can lead to not being able to hold people's attention.

- Past experiences: People may make assumptions about a person or situation based on what has happened in the past, impacting how they interact.

- Hidden agendas: Manipulation is used by the speaker in order to achieve their desired outcome.

- Status: Nerves and anxiety may influence how well we are able to express ourselves around those with a higher status.

- Stereotypes: Stereotypes are always dangerous, but when we make an assumption about a type of person, it changes our perspective. Just because a homeless person is poor, it doesn't mean they aren't educated and articulated.

Have you ever seen the challenge where people sit in a row blindfolded? The first has a huge bucket of water, and the last has a glass. The size of the container gets smaller for each person in the row. The goal is to pour the water from the first bucket over your head into the next person's bucket. Of course, blindfolded, this is difficult, but hopefully, there is enough water to eventually fill the glass.

Breakdowns and barriers in communication are a little bit like the water being passed into the buckets. A small amount of water is lost each time, but in the end, there is next to nothing left.

One misunderstanding may seem harmless on the surface, but the consequences spread. Misinterpretations, rumors, and gossip severely impact all types of relationships. If this happens in the workplace, there could be missed opportunities and financial losses.

Furthermore, ineffective communication leads to a ton of unsolved problems. The stress that comes with lingering issues can affect our sleep and motivation and, in turn, develop into anxiety.

Anxiety causes increased heart rate, blood pressure, and extra strain on the heart. This can increase the risk of heart disease. The same can be said for social anxiety, which is another reason why improving social skills is crucial, not just for mental health but also for physical well-being.

After all this information, you might be feeling like there is no hope considering the importance and complexity. Small steps in the right direction toward effective communication are what will break down these barriers.

What Effective Communication Looks Like

Effective communication is the ability to express ideas and concepts so that the listener fully understands them and that they take action. It also means that you are able to listen, decipher the message, and act upon it.

This is actually more complicated than it was in the past because there are so many more ways that we communicate. Instant messages, email, and business communication apps do a great job of keeping people connected, but it makes effective communication more challenging because we remove the personal aspect— there is no tone of voice or body language.

For this reason, we should look at both social and communication skills as something we have to continuously develop in order to be effective in the changing world. It sounds so simple, but things like proofreading an email and adding an emoji can completely change how a person receives a message.

When you master effective communication, you will be able to:

• Understand information from the onset.

• Build trust.

• Resolve problems and prevent them from escalating or even occurring.

• Provide your audience with direction.

• Strengthen relationships.

• Increase engagement and productivity.

• Create strong teams, whether in the home, educational institution, or workplace.

To achieve this, you can't just expect to have a better understanding of effective communication and wake up to be a pro. To get it right for every person and situation ahead of you, it's necessary to slow down and tackle one area at a time. We need to learn how to listen, how to organize our thoughts and actions, and how to make things interesting. We have to uncover the secrets of social cues and body language. And then, it's down to the art of conversation, initiating it, maintaining it, and making it meaningful.

All of this is going to begin with your confidence. When people are able to overcome shyness, awkwardness, and anxiety, they will have taken the first step to effective communication.

CHAPTER TWO: LAYING THE FOUNDATION FOR A CONFIDENT YOU

"I certainly have not the talent which some people possess," said Darcy, "of conversing easily with those I have never seen before. I cannot catch their tone of conversation, or appear interested in their concerns, as I often see done."

— JANE AUSTEN, *PRIDE AND PREJUDICE*

Anyone would who has seen the 2005 movie of this classic would look at the character of Mr. Darcy and think that he has it all, looks, style and, of course, wealth. But all of this is overseen as soon as he attempts a social interaction. Not only did he lack the skills, but he also had no confidence in himself.

There are four leads to confidence. Body language is the first thing someone may notice about us: the way we walk into a room or carry ourselves. Someone with a genuine smile, calm composure, and a firm handshake can ooze confidence.

Confident people have an element of positivity about them too. That's not to say that confident people force positivity, but they will look for the positive in a situation, and they have developed the ability to reframe their negative thoughts into more positive ones.

Confidence is one of the most important components of emotional intelligence. Going back to Mr. Darcy, he was obviously an intelligent man, but he lacked emotional intelligence, which made his social interactions even more awkward.

Being able to identify emotions enables you to understand social cues and pick up on potential tension. On the other hand, people with low emotional intelligence struggle to view their abilities and themselves in a positive way, impacting their communication skills.

The fourth factor of confidence is a growth mindset. A fixed mindset is one where a person believes that what they have in life now is all there is. A growth mindset is one where we are determined to learn and grow. We accept that mistakes are made, but from these mistakes, we can improve. It's these improvements that lead to confidence.

How to Be More Confident

We are going to jump straight into the practice with ways to start finding and improving your confidence before facing others and conversations.

Conquering your limiting beliefs

The human brain is wired to lean toward the negative. We look at our past, and it's easier to remember our negative experiences than our positive ones. But these negative experiences have a habit of sticking with us and shaping our adult selves.

Hugh Jackman explained how his parents divorced when he was young, and this experience stuck with him much like an injury would. He constantly had this feeling that the experience he had as a child would continue to cause him suffering. But if we keep telling the stories of our past, we are never going to break free from our limiting beliefs.

Before expecting to feel more confident, you need to recognize the beliefs that are holding you back and challenge them. By challenging them, you will see what is fact and what isn't. Then we can replace the false beliefs with those that empower us.

An example:

• My limiting belief: I will never be successful in an interview for a leadership role.

• Fact: I have had one unsuccessful interview.

• No evidence: Every interview I do will be bad. This is catastrophizing and fortune-telling.

• Empowering belief: If I take an online course on leadership, I will feel more confident in my abilities and more prepared for the next interview.

Connect confidence to your goals

Goals are a brilliant way to get the ball rolling with your confidence if you are setting goals the right way. People should have different goal categories. There will be long-term and short-term goals as well as personal and professional goals.

Every time you set a goal, it should be as specific as possible, including figures and numbers where appropriate. Your goals should be realistic. Using the Goldilocks Rule is a good way to decide whether a goal is attainable. The Goldilocks Rule states that to find your perfect level of motivation, the task at hand should be difficult enough to work hard but not so difficult that it is impossible.

Finally, make sure your goal has a time frame. It's no good to say that you will achieve your goal in the future. That's a given. But is that going to be in one month or six?

Once you have laid out the details of the goal, you need to break the bigger goal down into smaller steps. Each of these smaller steps should have a reward. Let's say you have a goal of paying off all of your debts in six months, and for this, you need $2,500 for two loans and three credit cards.

For each debt you pay off, you allow yourself a small treat. It doesn't have to be a financial reward; it could be cooking your favorite meal or starting the new series you have been saving.

Your confidence will start to grow once you hit your first milestone, providing you with momentum for the next.

Take credit for your achievements

Though we have seen that it is easier to look back at the negative, if you sit down and make the effort, you will be able to come up with a list of past successes. These could be exams you passed, obstacles you overcame, or even a moment when you stepped out of your comfort zone and things went better than you had planned.

Nobody is a complete failure, but when you are constantly comparing yourself to others, it can feel this way. Remember that everyone is on their own journey and what you see rarely portrays the real truth.

Another habit our limiting beliefs may cause is that when we look back at our past successes, we hand the credit over to other people involved. If your presentation was perfect, it's not because of the effort you made, but it was thanks to the person who set up the technology so that it all ran smoothly.

Next to your list of successes, write a sentence that takes credit for your achievements. This is an excellent reminder of what you are capable of.

Assess your top human need

Without direction, it's hard to feel confident. To discover your direction, you need to ask yourself one indispensable question. Why do you do what you do? We are all driven by our basic needs.

All humans need a sense of certainty to avoid possible pain and suffering. Certainty can lead us to do things we want to do as well as things we don't want to do. At the same time, humans also crave a level of uncertainty. After all, life would be rather boring with no variety.

We make many decisions to find significance in life because we want to know that we are important or special. This is especially challenging for those who avoid social situations and relationships. There is a close link between significance and the other human need, contributions, what gives our lives meaning.

Finally, we need love, connection, and growth. Understanding what your top needs are will help you find out more about where you want to go in life and concrete your goals.

Create healthy routines

A lack of routine can lead to poor sleep and eating, reduced physical health, and a tone of stress. What's more, you aren't using your time effectively, making it harder to achieve all you need to. None of these is going to instill a sense of confidence.

Begin with a healthy bedtime routine. Although it sounds like something we would tell our children, it's just as essential that adults get enough quality sleep. A routine before bed can include switching off from technology, herbal tea, breathing exercises, and trying to get to bed at the same time each night.

Avoid all technology in the bedroom. The blue light produced by screens prevents the release of melatonin, the sleep hormone.

Personally, I find a morning routine helps me to start the day in the right mood. Try getting up 10 minutes earlier and have a short workout, a healthy breakfast, and that first coffee of the day without rushing.

For your daily routine, ensure you are taking breaks. It's hard when there is so much pressure to get everything done, but short breaks are your chance to recuperate energy and calm the mind.

The perfect routine will include exercise. A 10-minute workout in the morning is a great start, but it won't add up to the recommended 150 minutes of moderate-intensity exercise. It sounds like a lot, but 10 minutes from Monday to Friday plus three 30-minute brisk walks, and you have hit your target!

Exercise is crucial for confidence and self-esteem. Not only will you feel more confident in your ability to communicate with others, but you will also start to feel less stressed and have more energy to accomplish more.

Practice gratitude

Expressing your gratitude can reduce those self-judging opinions of yourself. The ability to notice the good in your life and in others also improves self-esteem. One study showed that those who practiced gratitude had higher levels of empathy (Shi, 2020), which we have seen is fundamental in social interactions.

Here are some simple ways to start practicing gratitude:

• Journaling: Write down two or three things each day that you are grateful for.

• A gratitude jar: Write two or three things you are grateful for and pop them in the jar each day. When you are feeling down, randomly choose some papers to read.

• Gratitude walk: Turn your phone off and get outside. Pay attention to the things you see that you are grateful for.

• Gratitude meditation: Sit in a comfortable position and take a moment to focus on your breathing. For each exhale, think of something you are grateful for.

• Create a collage: Release your creative side and start collecting items and/or images to use in a collage. For example, a ticket from a concert, a dried flower someone gave you, photos of your family, or even of your pets.

Improve your self-talk and self-love

As harsh as it sounds, you are never going to find your confidence if you are constantly talking to yourself in a negative way. When we tell ourselves something often enough, it becomes true.

The trick is not to attempt to bury negative self-talk but to tackle it head-on. The first step is to distance yourself from the inner critic. Create a persona for your negative voice. You know it's easier to tell a friend how things really are than it is to tell yourself. This distance from your negative persona will help you challenge the critical voice and speak to yourself in the same kind of way as you would to a friend.

At the same time as challenging this critical persona, introduce some positive affirmations to your day. Just as the brain listens to the bombardments of negativity, it will also pay attention when you repeat positive statements. Examples of positive affirmations to improve your confidence include:

• I value myself.

• I believe in my abilities.

- I can face every challenge.

- I am succeeding in life.

- I am capable of greatness.

- I am a strong, unique individual.

- I am naturally confident and at ease with my life.

- I am totally confident in my path.

Positive self-talk is a necessary part of self-love. Those who are able to love themselves for who they are can reduce anxiety and depression while cultivating a positive mindset. If you don't love yourself, it's going to be hard to feel confident.

To increase your self-love, stop comparing yourself to others. It's easier than it sounds but think realistically, are you achieving anything by making comparisons? It's more likely that you are using energy that is better used for something that brings you benefits.

When you fall into the trap of comparing yourself to others, you start making subtle changes in order to be more like them. Each change chips away at your authenticity. Being true to yourself is empowering, and empowerment is a real confidence booster.

Improving your confidence will take some time, but it is always best to start with these techniques before working on confident conversations. Just planting the seeds of confidence will help those initial first steps.

Imagine your confidence as a snowball in an avalanche. As you practice these techniques, your golf ball-sized snowball slowly develops into the size of a tennis ball as it begins its journey down the mountain. With even a tennis ball of confidence, you will feel better talking to others as you continue to pick up momentum.

Approaching Conversations with Confidence

There is never going to be a perfect moment to break out of your comfort zone and start a conversation. Waiting for the ideal time is a form of procrastination, and you will end up talking yourself out of it.

Prior to initiating a conversation, at least as your confidence is still growing, prepare yourself physically and mentally. Amy Cuddy, a body language researcher at Harvard University, has identified high-power poses and low-power poses. Low-power poses include hunched shoulders, crossed arms, and looking down.

A saliva test from people who used high-power, open, and relaxed poses showed 20 percent more testosterone and 25 percent less stress hormone, cortisol (Clear, 2018). The ultimate power pose is the superhero pose, standing with legs slightly open, hands on hips, and chest open. However, you may want to do this away from the public eye!

In terms of mental preparation, just be a little more compassionate toward yourself. No human is perfect, and it's okay to make mistakes. Remember that it is better to get out there and try and make a mistake than to never try at all, as this will definitely lead to failure.

Here are five simple tips to have in mind as you start approaching conversations with more confidence:

1. Immediately start with trust. A smile, a firm handshake, and comfortable levels of eye contact will put someone at ease. Don't forget that there is a good chance that they are having the same doubts about their communication skills.

2. Build a rapport with the person. Respect them enough to give them your full attention, and watch out for your eyes wandering around the room.

3. Pause before you respond. It only has to be a second or two, but it will give the impression that you think before you speak.

4. Start with small talk but be sure it's an open-ended question that doesn't lead to a yes or no answer. Start your question with a who, what, where, when, or why.

5. Don't forget to keep smiling, keep making eye contact, and breathe!

So, you have started the conversation. Now how do you keep it going with confidence?

23 Tips to Feel Confident Talking to Anybody

This section can be used as a checklist for confident conversations. I don't recommend that you attempt to achieve each one straight away. Your brain will be so overwhelmed with remembering what to do that you won't be able to pay full attention to the conversation or the person. Instead, choose two or three and start practicing them with each conversation until they become natural.

- Slow down your speech so you don't appear nervous.

- Accept that feeling nervous is not a sign that you are in danger.

- Don't assume you know what the other person is thinking about you. They don't have the same view of yourself as you do.

- Keep your mind focused on the topic, and don't let it wander.

- Keep your mind focused on others and not your own "performance."

- Vary your tone to sound more relaxed.

- Create a persona for your nervousness to create distance.

- Plan for and practice conversations with people who make you nervous.

- Ask sincere questions to show your interest.

- Check the other person's feet. If they are pointing toward you, they are happy in the conversation. If they are pointing away, wrap it up.

- Offer information about yourself.

- Recognize that moments of awkward silence are not only your fault.

- Accept that short moments of silence are natural in conversations.

- Don't be scared of revisiting previous topics.

- Stand up straight and mentally check your posture throughout the conversation.

- Relax your facial muscles (practice this in a mirror to see the difference).

- Use the words "I'm not certain" or "I'm unsure" instead of a tone of voice that implies you are uncertain.

- Project your voice to be heard clearly but don't be the loudest person in the room.

- When speaking louder, lower your pitch slightly.

- Give verbal and nonverbal signals that you are listening. Add a "Really!" or "Yes" or nod every now and again.

- Use moments when you think to break eye contact so that this body language doesn't become too intense.

- Smile when appropriate but don't smile all the time, or else it will come across as fake.

- Reflect on conversations once they are over. Highlight what you did well and what can be improved.

It's a good idea to make this checklist a goal. This way, achieving your goal will also improve your confidence. Break the list of 23 items into groups of 4 or 5, and set yourself a small reward for each set you achieve.

Confidence makes you feel better and comfortable about who you are, and when you can approach strangers and openly talk to them, you dissolve that sense of awkwardness.

However, there can be certain aspects that, despite confidence, might limit you from facing social situations, such as anxiety. Let's tackle those next, shall we?

Defeating Social Anxiety

Social anxiety is a disorder where people are extremely overwhelmed by social situations. It often begins in teenage years, but events in your life can cause the disorder to present at any stage in life. For example, many felt the symptoms of social anxiety after the COVID pandemic and lockdowns.

People with social anxiety worry about everyday social interactions, from meeting people to speaking on the phone. Emotionally, they might feel embarrassed, like they are constantly being judged, and have low self-esteem. Physically, they may blush, sweat, feel sick, have a pounding heart, or suffer from panic attacks.

The first thing to do is to understand what it is that triggers your social anxiety. Some people feel immense panic at parties or when meeting new people. For others, it could be when they have to give a presentation or other occasions where they are the center of attention.

From here, you can break down that trigger into smaller actions so that the bigger picture isn't giving you so much stress. If you have to run errands, you might start to feel anxious about the five places you have to visit before leaving your home. Look at the five places individually and prepare yourself for each one. This is a similar process to a treatment used for social anxiety.

One of the most popular treatments for social anxiety disorder is cognitive behavioral therapy (CBT), which helps to reframe negative thought patterns.

Exposure therapy is a cognitive behavioral therapy technique that helps people overcome their fears. Exposure therapy can be in vivo (directly facing fears), imaginal (creating images of the fear), or virtual reality (using technology).

Exposure therapy can be graded, meaning the fear is broken down into smaller steps, and a person gradually faces their fears in smaller steps. It can also be flooded. In this case, exposure starts with the biggest difficulty.

For example, if you had a fear of public speaking and chose the in vivo gradual method, the steps would be to prepare the presentation and practice with a friend or family member, then to practice with two or three people. Then a small group with a stranger, and so on.

Beware of negative coping strategies. You might think that a glass of wine or two will help ease those nerves when facing your social anxiety, but this is rarely the case. Alcohol and drugs are short-term fixes and, over time, will only cause more harm. Both can make the symptoms of anxiety worse.

Overcoming Shyness

Being shy is often seen as a negative or a character flaw, but this is not the case—no more than you would say an introvert or extrovert has flaws. Some believe that shyness is genetic, while others feel that it stems from life experiences.

It may also be a simple case of an introvert being overly exposed to people and withdrawing from social interactions. On the other hand, extroverts can also be shy. These people love to be part of social events, but it takes them longer to warm up to people.

Just because you are shy doesn't mean you can't enjoy meaningful conversations in all social interactions. But it is important to recognize that being shy often means that you may overestimate the negative. We all assume that people are thinking the worst of us, but shy people take this to a whole new level.

A bit of tough love, but we have to take responsibility for this. These are our own negative thoughts overruling logic and evidence. If there are people in your life that genuinely think badly of you or mock your shyness, do you need them in your life? For other negative thoughts on how people view you, you need to go back to challenging these thoughts.

After challenging these negative thoughts, it's time to put a more positive spin on the conversations and situations you are about to face. Visualize yourself in the situation and image what you are doing and saying for things to go well.

If you are shy, give yourself a role in the situation you are about to face. Years ago, I would give myself the role of detective. By tasking myself with finding out about others, there was less room for me to focus on myself and my feelings. I felt that I had a sense of purpose and, at the same time, I was learning more about others, which helped a lot when it came to small talk.

Now that you have given yourself a dose of tough love, remember that you also need to give yourself a little bit of grace. Don't punish yourself for being shy. Switch thoughts like "I am shy" to "I am learning to be confident."

And remember that being shy comes with a lot of positive characteristics. These characteristics include thoughtfulness, intelligence, and being a good listener. Remind yourself of these qualities and what these attributes bring to a conversation.

What to Do When You Are an Introvert

While a shy person tends to fear more what the outside world thinks and feels, an introvert will turn their thoughts and feelings inward. Social interactions are often draining because an introvert spends so much energy processing their surroundings and the people in them.

The challenge with social situations is that an introvert has to force themselves to step out of their inner selves and interact with people around them.

To start becoming more confident with conversations and social interactions, begin by eliminating as much of the unexpected as possible. Life is never going to be that simple but begin by spending more time interacting with those who are familiar to you.

Often, this will be home and the workplace, areas that tend to be more structured. It's a good idea to invite friends and colleagues into your space rather than you venturing into theirs. In your own space, you will feel more in control.

When it comes to dealing with the unfamiliar, let's start with people. You are only half of a conversation, and you can't predict what they will say. However, you can prepare your side of the conversation and even play out different scenarios depending on what they might say. Some scripts will be easier to plan, such as ordering takeout.

The more complex topics may need some more research. If you have to attend a work function and you know the office is hot on politics, it's worth paying attention to the news so that you are more familiar with the topic.

For those events you know are going to push you to your limits, take an understanding friend along with you. Try not to rely on them for every challenging moment, but you could have a signal that allows them to step in when conversations become too much.

Try hard not to overuse your friend's presence. Naturally, they won't mind, but by making small efforts to overcome the obstacles being an introvert brings, you will start to feel that confidence and have more determination to tackle other areas of your social difficulties.

Interactive Element: Activities to Keep Social Anxiety And Stress at Bay

Regardless of being nervous, shy, introverted, or panicking when social occasions come up, there are strategies to help you when even the idea of social interactions is enough to overwhelm you, cause your heart to race, and a challenge to catch your breath.

We have looked at understanding your social anxiety, what to do, and what not to do. These practical exercises can help you manage the symptoms of social anxiety before they take control of you:

1. Use the 4/7/8 breathing technique

This technique involves inhaling for 4 seconds, holding for 7, and exhaling for 8. It doesn't have to be those exact times but make sure your exhale is longer than your inhale.

Controlled breathing helps to stimulate the vagus nerve. This nerve plays a major role in the parasympathetic nervous system (PNS). The PNS is what calms us down when we face danger or perceived danger in the case of social anxiety. Rather than remaining in flight or fight response, controlled breathing helps the body return to "rest and digest."

2. Practice progressive muscle relaxation

Progressive muscle relaxation is excellent because you can do it anywhere. Start with one group of muscles, for example, the feet. Tense and relax the muscles. Move your way up to the calf muscles and do the same. Slowly, work your way through the different sets of muscles in your body.

It's not possible for the body to be tense and relaxed at the same time. Intentionally tensing muscles and then releasing them brings about a relaxed sensation.

3. Use a grounding exercise

This grounding exercise helps to bring your mind back to the present by paying attention to your senses. It cannot only help with signs of anxiety but also during a panic attack. First, take some deep breaths, then:

- Find 5 things you can see.

- Find 4 things you can touch.

- Find 3 things you can hear.

- Find 2 things you can smell.

- Find 1 thing you can taste.

If these techniques don't make a difference after some time, please don't hesitate to see a professional, as there is no shame in this. Your anxiety might be so deeply rooted that you need some help to unravel it.

At the beginning of this chapter, we saw how body language was a major factor in confidence, but then it seemed that we ignored the subject. This wasn't the case because body language and nonverbal communication are so crucial that they deserve their own chapter.

4. Try a wall push

If your senses are being overloaded in a social situation (there is too much noise or the lighting is too bright), a wall push can help you feel more stable.

Keep your feet flat on the ground and your entire body up against a wall, even your palms. Push yourself against the wall for 5 to 10 seconds.

It also helps if you close your eyes for those seconds to give your brain a break from the stimuli.

5. Find your anxiety-relieving pressure points

Acupuncture is a traditional form of Chinese medicine, and while you aren't about to start sticking needles in yourself, you can apply pressure to specific parts of the body to relieve anxiety.

1. The hall of impression point: between your eyebrows, gentle circular movements for 5 to 10 minutes.

2. The heavenly gate point: the upper hollow part of your ear, circular pressure for 2 minutes.

3. The shoulder well point: on the shoulder, use the thumb and index finger to massage the front and back of the muscles firmly for 4 to 5 seconds.

4. The union valley point: the webbing between your thumb and index finger; apply firm pressure for 4 to 5 seconds.

Number 4 shouldn't be used if you are pregnant, as it can induce labor.

6. Practice rationalizing your thoughts

Below, you will find some irrational thoughts that may come about when you are socially anxious. It doesn't mean to say that these feelings aren't real for you, but there is no evidence to support them. Write a rational counterstatement for each one:

• My boss is going to complain about my work . . .

• My friends will laugh at my new outfit . . .

• The stranger is going to think I am stupid . . .

Now write down some of your own anxiety-producing thoughts and consider the rational approach.

These setbacks to our social and communication skills are just starting points on this journey. The moment you start to feel more in control of your emotions, the more you'll act and think accordingly, no matter the social situation.

Talking about actions, it's time to address the nonverbal elephant in the room . . .

CHAPTER THREE: NONVERBAL COMMUNICATION 101 – THE SCIENCE OF BODY LANGUAGE

"Language is a more recent technology. Your body language, your eyes, your energy will come through to your audience before you even start speaking."

— PETER GUBER

G uber's quote doesn't seem to make much sense at first. Before any technology, there was language, wasn't there? But, when we fully understand and learn how to use our body language, it will get the message across far better than any technology can. When your body language and your message don't match, regardless of your energy, the message will be mixed.

The ability to read social cues and improve your own will lead to results far more reliable than technology. Never can you guarantee that all electronic components will work when you need them. But your nonverbal language isn't going anywhere—once you master it!

Recognizing Social Cues

Social cues make up a large part of our communication—the nonverbal part. How much exactly is debated by professionals. Experts tend to agree that between 70 and 93 percent of communication is nonverbal (Spence, 2020).

Why such a difference? Well, our social cues communicate feelings, intentions, and reactions with or without words. Our brains' neurotransmitters pick up on social cues at an incredibly fast pace, often before we have the time to process what these messages are telling us.

This is why people can walk into a room and instantly not like a person before they have even been introduced. That's not to say that a relationship won't develop with the help of verbal communication, but that first impression based on nonverbal social cues has made an impact.

Social cues are similar across the world, but that's not to say they are universal. Let's take a look at 16 of the most common social cues, and you will be able to see how they can be subtly different from culture to culture, even from person to person.

1. Eye contact

2. Posture

3. Angling the body

4. Facial expressions

5. The tone of voice

6. The tone of the text

7. Silence

8. Paralanguage

9. Physical touch

10. Fidgeting

11. Gestures

12. Mirroring

13. Proxemics

14. Clothing

15. Seeming distracted

16. Volume.

Some of these, we have already discussed, like how to get comfortable with silence and how to adjust the volume of our voice to project more confidence. Clothing, too, matters. Aside from dressing for comfort, the clothes you choose will add to the impression you want to make.

Before diving into the intricacies of social cues, it's important to know how to start reading other people's body language.

Our first lessons of social cues begin when we are born, as without language, it's our first way of communicating. Babies start to mirror their role models, not just with gestures, body language, and expressions but also with tone of voice, even if the sounds are just babbling. As children grow up, social cues are developed through play.

Some of the reasons for not being able to read social cues stem from childhood, whether because there weren't enough role models or because of a lack of social interactions. Some children whose families move around a lot find this difficult because they aren't always in a place for long enough to develop friendships and play.

A number of health conditions are also linked to poor social cues. Autism, ADHA, and some learning disabilities are examples. Those suffering from social communication disorder will struggle with both spoken language and reading social cues.

Let's take this a step further by taking a closer look at body language in conversations.

What Your Body Is Telling Others

Our body language reveals more of our emotions and feelings than words alone. In some cases, it can even give the audience a more accurate understanding of what you are feeling. It's not just about how we move our body, but it comes down to our microexpressions that can't be controlled, the sounds we make, and how close we stand to other people.

Being more aware of what you do with your body will help you identify the same nonverbal cues that others are displaying. This connection is essential for earning each other's trust as well as ensuring your messages are accurately presented.

Something as simple as paying attention to the distance between people, known as proxemics, can literally make or break a conversation. Anything under 18 inches is considered an intimate space and reserved for people who have a close relationship. Even less than 4 feet can make someone feel uncomfortable because it is still a very personal distance.

Most of our social interactions should be between 4 and 12 feet. There is quite a distance here, but it tends to be shorter when people are more comfortable around each other.

The next time you have conversations with friends, family members, and acquaintances, pay more attention to how close you stand to each other. Get good at exploring what happens when you move closer. After the following sections, you will be able to sport peoples' discomfort and know when to back off slightly.

How to Read People's Faces

Our faces have the ability to express an incredible range of emotions, from pure shock to absolute joy. By looking at the eyes, nose, and mouth, we are able to see if somebody is trustworthy. Let's take a closer look at these parts of the face.

The Eyes

The right amount of eye contact can relax the other person and display confidence, but if you focus too much on the amount of eye contact, you might miss other cues.

Staring too intensely at someone might be a sign of dominance and intimidation. Frequently gazing in other directions is a sign of distractions and possibly boredom. A good rule of thumb is to maintain eye contact 50 percent of the time when talking, 70 percent of the time when listening, and for 4 to 5 seconds before breaking it. The goal is to make eye contact naturally, so use this as a rough guide.

A slow blink can indicate that someone is engaged in what you say, but when this is purposefully slowed down, it could mean the person feels your comment is a little stupid, and when someone tries not to blink, it's a common way of spotting a lie. This is often followed by rapid blinking because tension is being released. On the contrary, rapid blinking indicates stress.

Pupil dilation may take a little more practice to spot; however, it's a great sign to show that someone is pleased, interested, or even aroused. The bigger the pupils become, the more interested they are. Try showing someone different photos or videos and watch what happens to their pupils.

Finally, let's not forget what happens with the eyebrows. Typically, we would see raised eyebrows for happiness and surprise and lowered eyebrows for sadness and anger. When the eyebrows are frowned with tension lines between them, it's a sign of aggression. A single eyebrow raise, often accompanied by a head tilt, could imply disdain or support verbal communication, such as giving orders, demanding, or arguing a point of view.

Both or one raised eyebrow is a universal sign of skepticism. Another universal eyebrow sign is the flash, a quick raise that lets others know we are interested, possibly even physically.

The Mouth

A smile costs nothing but gives much—unless it's fake! A fake smile is an obvious sign of unhappiness, but it may also point to sarcasm and someone who is cynical. The way to tell a genuine smile is to look for crow's feet around the eyes.

If you notice someone with pursed lips when they are very tense, it could mean they are disapproving or distrustful. The more pursed, the more intense the feeling. Lip biting may have two meanings: stress or playful flirting. It's necessary to check for other cues like wide eyes and a smile to know the difference.

We often cover our mouths when we are shocked or surprised. It might also be a sign that someone is trying to cover their emotions, and on other occasions, we cover our mouths to stop ourselves from saying something—so a person might be holding something back.

The Nose

A wrinkled nose is a common sign of a bad smell, but this can be extended to other things we dislike. When nostrils are flared, a person might be preparing themselves for an altercation because the nostril can take in more oxygen.

Aside from touching or rubbing a nose when you have an itch, it may also mean that they don't believe what is being said. If the person is talking while they touch their nose, they might be lying, as they aren't comfortable with what they are saying.

Sometimes, people will stroke their noses, especially the bridge, as a way to release tension. We can also use our noses to lead someone's attention to a direction or object.

Bear in mind that some of these very subtle movements, or microexpressions, can't be controlled. Even with the most deliberate intentions, you can't control when your eyes dilate. For this reason, it's more crucial to control what you can, and this is true of other parts of the body.

Taking the Bigger Picture into Account

Nonverbal communication is like a recipe. All of the ingredients (or cues) work well on their own, but once you mix them all, you start to get the full spectrum of flavors. Recognizing individual cues is a great start, but when you can take in gestures from the entire body, you will get better at really uncovering people's hidden messages.

The Hands

We do a lot of "talking" with our hands, some cultures more than others. Waving, giving the thumbs up, and the okay hand gestures are fairly universal. Clenched fists are more often associated with tension and aggression.

Generally speaking, open hands with the palms facing up are a sign of openness and confidence. Confident people are also good at moving their hands in the space around their bodies without going to the extreme of waving them around. Steeple fingers are an excellent sign that someone is in control. It's very much a sign of power in the meeting room.

Going back to the palms, the direction and position of the palms make a difference. Turning your palms up when speaking can mean you are asking for a favor but turning them downward tends to imply a demand or order. A palm over your heart can show gratitude or sincerity.

At the same time, how we move our hands can support what we are saying, which is particularly helpful when explaining and giving instructions. When listing information, we can also show the corresponding fingers. If you want someone to take notes, you can pinch your thumb and index fingers and gesture writing.

Watch out for you and others fiddling with your hands. This gesture often indicates nerves, anxiety, and tension. If you notice someone else's hand fidgeting, you can try changing your body language to help put them at ease. Again, it could be as simple as moving a little further away. Rapid hand movements like tapping might mean the person is bored or frustrated.

Arms and Shoulders

Crossed arms have long been seen as a negative, closed-off position, but this isn't always the case. It's true that, combined with other cues like tension, this is a sign of being closed off. Folded arms are a gesture we pick up as young children as a form of protecting ourselves, a survival instinct to cover our vital organs.

Nevertheless, this could also signify that a person is comfortable when matched with a genuine smile and relaxed shoulders. Men may sit with crossed arms but open legs, which would imply more comfort than being defensive or closed off.

If someone's arms are crossed, and their hands are clenching the opposite arms, even to the extent that knuckles go white, the person might be feeling extreme tension, and this is a way of self-hugging themself. You might notice this position in a doctor's or dentist's surgery.

The most frequent type of shoulder shrug we use is brief and signals that we aren't sure or we don't understand. When shoulders remain raised, it's more likely that the person is feeling submissive. It's another action that points to protecting ourselves as the neck is less exposed.

The single-shoulder shrug is a playful gesture more often used by women to show their attraction to someone else. If it's not matched with other flirtatious signs, watch out for someone not telling you the truth. A partial shrug can suggest that someone isn't committed to what they are saying.

The Legs

In some ways, crossed legs are similar to crossed arms. In some cases, this is a sign of someone's discomfort and an attempt to protect themselves. But if you think of women who often wear skirts, this isn't necessarily the case. It might be just more comfortable for them.

Rather than just assuming crossed legs are a negative sign, pay more attention to the direction of the knees, ankles, and toes. When these body parts are pointing toward you, they are interested in what you are saying and probably want to hear more. If turned away from you, it's more likely they are disinterested or want some space. Follow the direction of the legs to see what is catching their attention.

The direction in which we move our legs also indicates interest. A leg moving toward you is a good sign but pulling the leg back signals a lack of interest.

Interestingly, how someone stands can indicate confidence. Normally, a confident stance with legs slightly apart, no more than shoulder width apart, is a sign of confidence. When the feet are wider than shoulder width, this is a way for people to take up more space, a territorial position.

Aside from body language, another part of the puzzle should coincide with our words and message. When we look at the difference between verbal and nonverbal, verbal consists of actual words. A part of nonverbal communication is the sounds we make, called paralanguage.

The Vocal Side of Nonverbal Communication

Paralanguage refers to secondary communication functions. This includes things like our tone and pitch of voice, which can increase when we want to emphasize keywords or at the end of a sentence to imply a question. A lower tone can imply a passive or submissive speaker. Being able to change the tone of voice during a conversation can help keep your audience engaged compared to a monotonous tone.

The speed of how we speak can point to excitement and happiness when we start to talk faster. According to the National Center for Voice and Speech, the average conversation speech in the English language is 150 words per minute (Barnard, 2018). At this speed, your message can be conveyed clearly and with confidence. While you aren't going to count the number of words you use in each minute, you can use a dictation app to give yourself an idea of what your average speed is.

Slowing down the speech may be a good idea to explain yourself more clearly, but if you start slowing down your talking too much, you can risk coming across as condescending or as if you are talking to people as if they are stupid.

There is also the question of volume. In some circumstances, you may have to raise your voice because of environmental or background noise. Getting the right volume sends out a confident message, whereas a little too loud and you may appear aggressive.

On the contrary, those who are quiet can appear to be shy, nervous, or anxious in social situations. They may not feel very confident when it comes to asserting their needs and wants.

The second side to paralanguage is the noises we make, or in some cases, don't make—in the case of silence. Bear in mind that the paralanguage in this section is based on the English language, and while some are universal or at least widespread, different cultures will have their own vocal sounds.

How we say what we say can have massive implications. Think of the different ways you can say "okay," along with some of the cues we have seen. Here are some examples:

- Okay with a smile and a nod.

- Okay with emphasis on the "O"

- Okay with emphasis on the "kay."

- Okay loudly with raised hands.

- Okay with a hug or stroking a shoulder.

- Okay with an eye roll.

We also have fillers that can show how much attention we are paying or not paying. Some of the positive fillers that express interest could be: "Uhh-hum," "Ahhh," and "Ohhh." Whereas fillers that sound like moans and groans can give a negative impression. A sigh can express boredom or frustration, and "Mmm" and "Errr" could signal that someone wasn't actively listening to your message.

Another more modern type of paralanguage comes in handy when we can't read these clues in person. Nonverbal messages are almost impossible to detect in written communication, but with the use of emojis, stickers, and emoticons, we are able to imply a tone to the message. Going back to the different ways we can say okay, scroll through your recent emojis and see how various images could change the way this word is interpreted.

How do you master all of these nonverbal cues? It's actually quite simple. First of all, while there are a lot of cues here, nobody expects you to remember everything at once, so don't panic about information overload.

Next time you're out there, engaging with someone, just make a mental note of the way their body and expressions change. You don't have to remember all the details. Start small and then expand. Then, reflect on these later so that you can better understand what that person was actually trying to say during your conversation.

It's a good way to keep this habit as long as it takes for you to recognize cues from the get-go. And you don't have to overwhelm yourself—start with one person to keep mental notes, preferably someone you know, and then slowly move ahead.

You can also try various cues in conversations, adjusting your mannerisms and gestures to reflect a particular meaning nonverbally and see how naturally others react to it.

There is one more way to tune into what someone else is talking about. And this involves using your ears—listening.

CHAPTER FOUR: TUNING IN TO WHAT OTHERS ARE SAYING

"We have two ears and one mouth, so we should listen more than we say."

— ZENO OF CITIUM

Not only is this one of my favorite quotes, but it is also one of the most obvious yet ignored quotes. So much emphasis is put on speaking, but without listening, how can we have a meaningful conversation?

What Does Listening Really Involve?

Listening is a process that involves receiving, interpreting, recalling, and evaluating verbal messages with the intention of responding appropriately.

This process doesn't occur in a linear fashion but can overlap. Add speed to the equation, and you can see how the process might get complex. We will start with an explanation of each part of the process.

Receiving

Our senses are constantly picking up on the stimuli in an environment, primarily from our auditory and visual channels. This is how we receive information, whether that's the visual cues we pick up from other people's body language, the tone of voice, and the spoken language people use.

This is an ongoing process throughout communication but remember that when it comes to phone calls, texts, and emails, the visual aspect is missing. At the same time, some audio disturbances can interrupt how we receive information. This could be background noise like chatter and music, environmental noise like traffic, and even psychological noise caused by stress.

Interpreting

During interpretation, the brain takes in all of the stimuli and starts making sense of them. At this stage, we put the information into context and relate it to previous experiences. The brain can compare this new information with old information and make updates and revisions if our new information is accurate and relevant.

We may have difficulties interpreting information if we lack previous experience. When this happens, it's not as easy to transfer information to our long-term memories, which leads us to recall.

Recalling

It is estimated that we forget almost half of what we hear immediately after hearing it. Even more could be forgotten if you aren't interested in the subject. How we recall the information we have heard depends on our memory storage units.

Sensory storage has the ability to recall large amounts of information but for a short time—as little as a tenth of a second for visual information and around 4 seconds for auditory stimulation. During the interpretation process, information gets sent to the short-term memory. Short term really is short, storing that information for up to 1 minute. Once enough neuro connections have been made, this information is then stored in the long-term memory.

We also have a working memory. This type of storage allows the brain to store and process information simultaneously, meaning we don't have to tap into our long-term memory to access the information. This is essential for listening because we can process information as new stimuli are introduced.

Evaluating

In this process, we decide if the information is credible, complete, and of value. Our brain is analyzing whether the information is true, if there is something that needs to be read between the lines, and establishing if the information is good or bad, right or wrong. To do this, we need critical thinking skills.

When you combine critical thinking skills with listening skills, you are able to take a more active role in communication. The trick here is not to get too obsessed with the evaluation stage because this could inhibit the ability to take in new information from the speaker.

Responding

As we saw in the previous chapter, our response can be verbal and nonverbal. From the last chapter, we learned how things like paralanguage and gestures show a person we are listening to them. These are known as back-channel cues. Other back-channel cues like fidgeting and looking away indicate that a person isn't listening.

Paraphrasing is a verbal response to someone. People do this by rephrasing what has been said to show they understand, to ask a question for clarification, or to ask a question for more information.

Paraphrasing is crucial when nonverbal communication is limited, for example, in a text message, to reduce miscommunications.

Listening is essential for our academic and professional success as well as our relationships. It doesn't matter what social situation we are in. If we can't listen, we can't empathize!

People have different listening styles, although it's rare to find someone whose style is limited to just one. See if you can relate to any of the following styles:

People-oriented listeners

These types of people are worried about the well-being of others and known to be good listeners. They are empathetic, which means they often have careers caring for others. These types of listeners may be easily distracted from their task if they know someone is in need.

Action-oriented listeners

You can imagine these people as those who like their information to be a matter of fact, without waffle, well organized, and accurate.

It's a great style for logistical types of careers. However, because they are keen on action, they might not be as keen or patient to fully listen.

Content-oriented listeners

They thrive on complex messages and understanding multiple perspectives. Often, they will ask questions to ensure they are being as thorough as possible, and this makes them suitable for careers in the sciences, law, and politics.

They might struggle with this thoroughness when it comes to tasks that need to be completed within a time frame.

Time-oriented listeners

As the name implies, these listeners are concerned with time limits and following a set time frame. They like information to be presented so they can come to quick decisions.

Time-oriented listeners tend to verbalize their time restrictions and are more inclined to use nonverbal cues to emphasize their sense of urgency.

As we are working through this chapter, keep these listening styles in mind and decide which skills you are skilled in and which you might need to work on. With this in mind, let's look at what it takes to be an active listener.

What Is Active Listening?

Active listening is when you are completely listening to a person using all of your senses, and verbal or nonverbal cues are given to show the speaker that you are fully paying attention. It's a skill that can be developed, but it does require a conscious decision to do so!

To actively listen to someone means that you don't jump into comments or questions, even when there are a few seconds of silence, as this could be a time the speaker needs to gather their thoughts. It's about not feeling the need to judge, form opinions, or offer unsolicited advice. So as well as listening, there has to be an element of self-control.

We have seen how smiling, eye contact, posture, and mirroring are nonverbal cues to show we are actively listening. We also know that fiddling with your watch, clothes, or even touching parts of the body are signs that you aren't listening.

For verbal signs that we are actively listening, it's important to remember particular details to show that information has been absorbed. We can combine this with positive reinforcement, words such as "Good," "Yes," or "Great." You can also reflect on what they say, ask questions to clarify or summarize what has been said.

In the next conversation you have, try putting some of these techniques and responses into action:

• Building trust and rapport: "What can I do to help you?" "Your presentation was really impressive."

- Demonstrating concern: "It must be hard for you right now." "How are your family coping?"

- Paraphrasing: "So you aren't sure you can make it on Saturday." "You think it's a better idea that we delay the meeting until 5."

- Short affirmations: "You need more time to do this." "Thank you for letting me know."

- Asking open-ended questions: "How long before you finish your assignment?" "What would you prefer for dinner?"

- Waiting to offer your opinion: "Tell me more about how you would do it." "Can you give me some more information about your idea?"

- Sharing similar situations: "I felt the same after my divorce." "I didn't know how to handle the boss either."

If you try to attempt all of these in one conversation, you will end up passively listening rather than actively listening because your mind will be too focused on what to do next rather than what the speaker is telling you. That being said, there are other obstacles when it comes to active listening.

Bad Listening Practices

Within communication, not everything is in our control. Nevertheless, there are some things that we can stop straight away and instantly become better listeners.

The first is interrupting. Conversations generally have a natural flow, and when a person starts interrupting, this flow is broken. Sometimes, our interruptions are accidental and caused by misreading cues, which you will get better at. If you do interrupt, an apology can make all the difference.

Be careful not to fall into the habit of aggressive listening. People listen with the sole intention of attacking what the speaker says. The first problem is that you might not be listening to the whole message, filtering only what you want to hear. The second is that your build-up of frustration can cause them to feel insecure.

Narcissists need to be the center of attention. This is no different from narcissistic listening, and a person will always try to bring a conversation back to them. They can do this by interrupting or one-upping.

Pseudo-listening is when a person gives all the right cues that they are paying attention, but they aren't actually listening. They won't be able to remember what was said and will often give an irrelevant response.

The following barriers can get in the way of active listening, and by being aware of them, we are more prepared to overcome them.

Barriers to Active Listening

During every listening process and for every listening style, there is a risk of barriers to active listening. First of all, it is natural for us to have to overcome some physical and environmental barriers.

Lighting and temperature are two examples. If a room is too dark and/or warm, we can feel tired. Too bright or cool, and it might make us uncomfortable. This is especially the case for autistic people who have sensory challenges.

Even the position of furniture in a room can cause distractions, especially in a professional setting where we can't see the main speaker.

Physical barriers are physiological noises, those that come from inside us. Imagine how much harder it is for you to fully listen when you are in pain, or you are suffering from a cold or other illness. Another type of physical barrier is psychological noise. Our mood and stress levels can deeply impact our ability to actively listen.

While you might think that this refers to negative moods, it's equally common with positive moods. If you have ever been in love or extremely excited about something, it's hard to keep your mind on anything else.

Some barriers combine the two, such as fatigue, because there are elements of stress and weakness from being tired. When anxiety presents with physical symptoms like shaking, you also have a combination of barriers.

And yet barriers are there to be broken, so don't let these be reasons not to actively listen. In fact, just being aware of these barriers can help you improve your listening skills. Preempting a colleague or classmate that you aren't feeling well can prevent them from assuming you aren't paying attention or aren't interested. Still, there are more ways you can get better at this skill and, at the same time, overcome the barriers.

Becoming a Better Active Listener

Because we are all so different, some people will find techniques more beneficial than others. It's a good idea to work your way through these techniques and make a note of the impact they made on your listening skills.

1. Creating an internal dialogue

It might seem like talking to yourself is counterproductive but start by firmly telling yourself that you are being distracted. Reinforce yourself by reminding your brain that you are implementing your listening skills and that this will be beneficial. Finally, remind yourself how active listening in the moment is going to help.

2. Mental boxing

In your mind, separate the thoughts that are relevant to the message from those that are distracting and intrusive. When you feel your mind drifting to what you want for dinner, put that intrusive thought in a box.

3. Use mnemonic devices

Using things like acronyms (My Very Educated Mom Just Served Us Noodles to remember the names of the planets) and rhymes (turn me right to make me tight) are techniques to help you recall information. Visualizing the information can also help.

4. Take notes

Not only will your notes help you recall information later, but the practice shows the speaker that you are focused and engaged. At the same time, if there is something you don't understand, ask for clarification.

5. Listening for the complete meaning

There are two parts to each message. One is the content, and the other is the emotions or attitudes toward the content. Understanding the emotions and attitudes come from verbal and nonverbal cues, and an active listener will respond to these cues to establish empathy. Verbalize your feelings to show you have listened and understood.

6. Practice mindful listening

Take a moment to sit quietly with your eyes closed. Listen to every detail you can hear, whether it's the hum of a fridge or children playing outside. When intrusive thoughts appear, don't try to push them away but let them pass and bring your attention back to listening.

7. Avoid prejudice and bias

Being impartial means you don't judge people before giving them a chance to speak. These prejudices lead us to make assumptions about the message without even listening to it. Someone who is using too many jazz hand movements might not be trying to dominate the space. They might be incredibly nervous and trying to overcompensate!

8. Put yourself in their shoes

This is an incredible way to truly empathize with the speaker. You can gain new perspectives and better understand the emotions rather than just the message. It also helps us to be more open-minded, remove any prejudice, and practice patience with the speaker— something you hope others would do for you. Remember that empathetic listening takes time.

9. Use the HURIER method

The HURIER acronym is an essential device to help you remember the core elements of active listening. HURIER stands for Hearing, Understanding, Remembering, Interpreting, Evaluating, and Responding.

You will now have noticed that a crucial part of active listening is the ability to tap into the emotional message. This, along with reading cues, is going to help you recognize when there are contradictions in communication. That being said, we have yet to cover how to actually intentionally listen to the message.

How to Listen with Intent

Listening with intent creates a sense of inclusion like you are part of something rather than hoovering on the outside, and this leads to a feeling of safety. When a person feels safe in their surroundings, they are better able to retain information. What's more, the insights you gain will lead to better decision-making.

We have seen how aggressive listening is negative but think about it from the viewpoint of intention. Is your intention to understand what needs to be done in a meeting, or is your intention to find fault in your coworker or prove your ideas are better?

Even if you are only thinking that their ideas are ridiculous and not verbalizing your thoughts, you are still not actively listening. Furthermore, by now, you might realize that your body language is giving away your thoughts!

To listen with the intent of understanding the message, you should:

- Prepare yourself to listen. Calm your mind and remove thoughts that aren't appropriate to the matter at hand.

- Remove any biases straightaway. How many times have you sat down to listen to someone and thought, "This is going to be boring?" You don't know this!

- Make the speaker feel comfortable. This will help them deliver a message with more clarity.

- Focus on the speaker. A good tip is to have a look around a room as soon as you enter it. That way, when it comes to listening to the speaker, you can keep your eyes directed at them.

- Allow the person to finish each point before you ask a question. They may already have the answer to your question but haven't had the chance to finish.

- Provide them with feedback. Use the nonverbal cues we practiced in the previous chapter to show you understand. For example, keep your knees or feet pointing in their direction.

- Be kind and supportive. Nowadays, too often, we are quick to find fault instead of praising people for their successes.

Put this into practice today. Your goal in the next conversation you have is to simply stop talking! Remind yourself that you have one mouth and two ears, and listen! Although you need to practice your body language, just for the next conversation, forget this so that the mind is more focused. Be strict with yourself. The only things that can come out of your mouth are fillers to show you are listening, questions for clarification, and paraphrasing with a focus on their emotions.

Evolving to Become a Reflective Listener

Reflective listening ties all of our points together so that you and the other person know they have been heard and understood and that the outcomes have been achieved. During a conversation, we need to reflect on the content, feelings, and meaning by using an appropriate combination of the skills we have learned.

Rather than reemphasizing these skills, let's look at a conversation in action where Emma is the reflective listener and Sophie is the speaker. Sophie is getting married in a week and is feeling incredibly overwhelmed.

• Sophie: "I am so stressed out, and I'm not sure if I can cope with all that still has to be done." (Notice that Sophie's shoulders are tense, her gaze is downward, and she is fidgeting with her engagement ring. Her tone of voice is low, she is quiet, and her voice is almost trembling.)

• Emma: "This must be awful." (Moves closer and gently rubs Sophie's back for comfort.) "What do you need?"

• Sophie: "The flowers still need to be collected. I haven't organized all the gifts. My mom is freaking me out about the food, and now I'm not sure I made the right choice with the band."

• Emma: "Okay." (Nodding in a reassuring tone. Not interrupting, and giving Sophie the chance to finish.)

• Sophie: "I want to be excited, and this should be a happy week, but I'm tired. I still have two days at work, and my boss is being awkward. I just need to sleep!"

• Emma: "So, you need to sort out the flowers and the gifts while calming down your mom, reminding yourself why you chose this band, and getting through work."

• Sophie: "Yes."

• Emma: "You know that I have never been married, so I can't pretend to know how you are feeling, but I do have an anxious mom. Can I offer you some advice?"

• Sophie: "Please!" (Notice that Sophie's body language has changed. She is more relaxed; she has turned toward Emma and is showing signs that she genuinely wants advice and isn't just being polite.)

• Emma: "When my mom starts to stress about something, I try to find tasks that take her mind off things and make her feel needed and important. Could she pick the flowers up for you?"

Naturally, the conversation would progress but notice how taking in the whole picture gives Emma the ability to reflect on Sophie's meaning and feelings. Rather than rushing in to solve a problem she doesn't fully understand, Sophie validates Emma's feelings and creates empathy. She asks questions for more information while keeping the focus on her friend, and she reads nonverbal cues to ensure she understands and is able to respond appropriately.

When you are actually tuned in to what others are saying, you engage yourself better in a conversation without using any judgment or preconceived notions, or indeed your ego, to complete what others are saying.

Well, so far, we have a good start. You know how to read nonverbal and body language cues, and you are well versed in actively listening to what others have to say.

This leaves the point of your own role in a dialogue—the very act of conversing. Keeping nonverbal cues and active listening close to your heart, let's dive headfirst into the art of making conversations, shall we?

CHAPTER FIVE: FIRST IMPRESSIONS AND A CONVERSATION ENTRÉE

"The first impression is readily received. We are so constituted that we believe the most incredible things; and, once they are engraved upon the memory, woe to him who would endeavor to efface them."

— JOHANN WOLFGANG VON GOETHE

The human mind is exceptionally fast at making judgments, and for good or bad, bias plays a role in our first impressions too. The halo effect, or first impression bias, is when we have a positive first impression of someone that tends to lead to automatically assigning feelings about a person in a different area.

For example, when somebody meets a beautiful person, the halo effect could cause them to believe that this person is kind and trustworthy. If someone turns up late, we associate this person with a lack of organization and professionalism.

One study showed that it took a fraction of a second for people to make judgments on attractiveness, likeability, and trustworthiness (Kelly, 2017). Considering the long-term implications of a first impression and the fact that there is no do-over, it's crucial to get it right.

So, What Really Is Conversation?

A conversation is usually an informal interaction between two or more people about a topic of interest. Put like that, it should be simple, but for many, starting and continuing a conversation can be challenging. It helps to think of conversations like a dance and, like most dances, there are rules to follow.

First and foremost, conversations are a two-way street, which goes back to the fact that we have two ears and one mouth, and a balance must be established. As much as we are used to broadcasting our opinions on social media, conversations should be an interaction of views and ideas.

Sometimes, when nerves take over, we can forget our manners. It is generally not polite to jump into conversations that could be problematic such as religion and politics, especially with strangers. It's also crucial that the things we say are nice. If you want to appear friendly, you can't begin conversations with gossip and unkind words.

Of course, a meaningful conversation will be one that combines our techniques from the previous chapters. Consider your body language, actively listen so that you can respond appropriately, and use emotional connections to establish a rapport.

By following the rules, we are able to experience feel-good conversations that are important for our mental health. Each minute, millions of chemical reactions occur in the brain, releasing dopamine, oxytocin, and endorphins. These happy hormones influence our mood and impact the relationship we have with someone.

Prior to a meaningful conversation, we need to ensure our audience is open to interactions, which requires a positive first impression.

Making a Good First Impression

Whether a first impression is accurate or not, it will last. Negative first impressions, whether through bias or your own wrongdoing, will make it harder for the person to overcome these initial opinions, and it will take longer for them to see you as trustworthy.

Enough about how things can go wrong. Let's look at 25 tips to make sure your first impression makes a difference.

1. Research ahead of time so that you know your audience and surroundings. It will help you choose the right language and provide you with conversation starters.

2. Check what you are wearing. Your choice of clothes should be appropriate for the occasion and can show your feelings toward an occasion.

3. Prepare a few things as a way to introduce yourself.

4. Consider the impression you want to make. How do you want others to feel about you?

5. Show respect with eye contact straight away and show warmth with a genuine smile. Add an eyebrow flash to show interest and happiness.

6. Repeat their name. Hearing their name activates a particular part of the brain and interests them, giving them a dopamine boost.

7. Start with a compliment to make the other person feel good about themselves.

8. Be yourself and try not to worry about what others are thinking. Trying to be someone you aren't for the sake of others is insincere and will be spotted.

9. Put your phone away. It's a distraction and shows a lack of respect.

10. Pay attention to your eyes and mouth, keeping those positive cues in action.

11. Don't judge people by their first impression, as they might be as nervous, if not more, as you. Be optimistic.

12. Keep your toes pointing toward the person, your arms relaxed next to your side, your shoulders down and back, and your chin parallel to the ground.

13. Make sure your hands are always visible.

14. Offer them something to hold like a drink or a business card. This helps them to open up crossed arms and remove barriers.

15. Lower your tone of voice but without exaggerating or sounding false.

16. Use sensory words to build rapport. People tend to favor one sense over others. If you hear a word like "I'm touched" or "I hear you," you can mirror these sensory words.

17. Match the adjectives they use. Listen for words like fantastic, amazing, and incredible. This is another way to build rapport.

18. Break the ice with appropriate humor. Helping others laugh releases happy hormones and can release any tension caused by nerves.

19. Mirror their energy levels. If someone is excited, be excited, and don't remain excited when the conversation tones down!

20. Chew gum—with your mouth closed and not in interviews! People who chew gum are viewed to have more positive traits.

21. When in a group and you see someone wanting to join the conversation, take a step back to let them in.

22. If you see someone who isn't talking to anyone, approach them.

23. Don't force yourself to make first impressions if it's not your day. If you are particularly anxious or depressed, you may not be able to overcome it.

24. Don't forget your last impression. End on a positive, both verbally and nonverbally.

25. Self-evaluate your first impression. What did you do well, and where are the areas to improve?

You might wonder why handshakes are not on the list. Since the pandemic, physical contact is almost seen as a faux pas. Whether you choose to shake someone's hand is going to be your personal preference, and you should also respect theirs. If there are no handshakes, you should still remember to keep your hands open, especially when you first meet someone.

Fortunately, with a lot of our interactions now online, we don't need to worry about handshakes. Nevertheless, this increase in digital interactions means we can't forget the first impression we make on screen.

When it comes to video calls, people seem to think that attire is not as important. We all know someone who thinks it's okay to jump into a meeting with no pants on. Still, dress appropriately, as this will keep you in the right mindset.

Ensure your background is free from distractions, and add lighting to brighten your face. There is such a thing as personal space online, so try to remain around 1.5 feet from the screen. Finally, look at your webcam and not the screen, particularly during introductions.

When it comes to your social media accounts and emails, always double-check for grammar and spelling mistakes. Mistakes can be a sign that you don't respect the person enough to check your text and can also draw attention away from the message.

Even with our best intentions, there may be times when your first impression doesn't go as well as you had hoped.

The first thing to do is not panic because there are ways you can still recover from this.

Ditch the usual questions you hear during first impressions, like where are you from and what do you do. Instead, try talking about something that spikes an interest. Food is always a good start because everyone has to eat. If there is no food, make a comment or ask a question about your environment. There will be more on small talk soon.

The bad impression may also be reversed simply by changing your settings, so try moving to a different area. Two of the simplest ways to undo the wrong are to ask for help and tell somebody that you like them. When you ask someone for help, they like you more; it's the psychological effect known as the Franklin Effect. And how happy do you feel when someone says, "I like you?"

If you feel like a person who's skilled at killing conversations, the next section will enable you to talk like a pro.

Conversation Starters That Ooze Confidence – Even With Strangers

So, you have prepared yourself mentally, are happy in your outfit and made it through the first impressions and introductions. What's next? How do you start a conversation? Before starting and maintaining conversations, it's wise to know how not to kill one.

As mentioned, avoid any type of conversation that involves strong opinions. Current affairs are topics most people are aware of due to the news and social media but jumping into a political debate can either kill a conversation or turn it into a heated one. Also, avoid things people could take offense to. This can include culture, race, ethics, and beliefs, not to mention offensive jokes.

The same can be said if you want to start a conversation with someone you are attracted to. While you might be tempted to try a pickup line you have heard of, it is often best to stick to a more direct approach, like asking if you can buy them a drink.

In all cases, never start a conversation with a negative. It will set the tone for the rest of the conversation and destroy any positive first impression you made. On a similar note, don't forget that your body language, emotional rapport, and listening skills don't end after the first impression!

A mistake you might make is to open the conversation with slang. Slang is fine in certain situations but certainly not when you are starting conversations, more so with strangers.

Avoid the most exhausting question ever: "How are you?" What happens? They say, "I'm fine, thank you, and you?" You reply with "Good," and the silence becomes awkward. Start with open-ended statements like "Tell me about yourself" so that you can listen for something in common. If nothing comes up, find a connection. If you are at a party, the chances are the same person has invited you, so ask how they know this person.

The same can be said for many of our conversation starters that have been recycled for decades. When you ask someone what they do, there is no effort or genuine interest.

You are likely to get a short answer about their profession. Instead, ask them how they stay busy. The response is more likely to include work, family life, and hobbies.

If it's someone you know, try not to open with "What have you been up to?" because the most common response is, "Nothing much." A statement like "Catch me up on life since I last saw you" encourages them to think a little deeper because, one way or another, things happen in our lives.

I can't stress enough how a compliment can be one of the best conversation starters. At the last wedding I attended, I overheard someone mention how lovely another person's shoes were. This led to a group of four or five people discussing shoe sizes, where they buy their shoes, matching socks, and so on. Without exaggerating, this group spoke for about 20 minutes—all because of one compliment.

It doesn't have to be related to clothes. Take advantage of your eye contact to complement their eyes or other aspects of their appearance. It could also be about the speech or presentation they gave or a witty comment they made.

Compliments are perfect icebreakers for strangers. Not only does it open the door to a conversation, but it also makes them feel good about themselves. Your words have given them a rush of happy hormones, and they will feel more positive about the rest of the conversation.

Paying compliments is particularly useful if English isn't your first language. This is because the vocabulary and sentence structures are all basic, and people can feel less self-conscious about their level of English.

At the same time, when people ask you these questions, you want to make sure your response is engaging and provides a chance to extend the conversation. Rather than only letting people know what you do for a living, give them a story with it.

For example, "I'm a chef, but I confess, I don't cook at home. In fact, I have the ability to burn toast in my own kitchen." You have provided the other person with at least two potential questions. Who cooks at home, and what types of food do you like cooking?

Next, you can combine these ideas with conversation starter inspirations for a variety of situations.

Conversation Starters by Topic or Situation

These are just some ideas to get the conversation ball rolling. Remember that for any situation, scan the environment first and use your senses to initiate conversations. If you really start to struggle, remember the FORD method for conversation starter topics: Family, Occupation, Recreation, and Dreams.

Approaching a stranger

- Do you know if there are any snacks here?

- What did you think of the talk/presentation?

- Is this your first time here?

- What's the most interesting thing you have learned here?

- Is your day going as expected?

- Can I help you with that?

At a party

- How do you know the people here?

- What made you come tonight?

- Where did you get your jacket from?

- What was the highlight of your day today?

- Have you ever been to a party like this before?

- How is your drink?

- Do you recommend any drinks?

Over dinner

- Have you tried the pasta here?

- What's the strangest thing you have ever eaten?

- What's your favorite type of cuisine?

- What is the most successful dish you have prepared?

- Do you know what kind of fish that is?

- Do you know much about wine?

Questions for students

- What are you most looking forward to this trimester?

- What's it like living with your roommate?

- What made you choose your course?

- Who is your most/least favorite professor?

- Have you explored the university facilities?

- What's your favorite study method?

When you need to network

- What was your first job?

- What made you choose your career?

- What department are you in?

- What interesting projects have you been working on lately?

- Do you get to travel with your job?

- How do you overcome the challenges in your job?

Dates and romantic interests

- What is your family like?

- What do you like to do on your day off?

- Tell me about your best friend.

- What was your last biggest achievement?

- What's the worst pickup line you have ever heard?

- What would be your perfect second date?

The ultimate conversation starters for any situation

- What's the best thing you've seen on Netflix recently?

- What is something that made you laugh today?

- What is your favorite social media site?

- Have you been anywhere interesting recently?

- Are you a cat person or a dog person?

- If you could only choose one food/song/movie for the rest of your life, what would it be?

- Would you rather visit a hot country or a cold country?

- What talent do you wish you had?

- What's the worst joke you have ever heard?

So, for a quick recap, first impressions take milliseconds to make but will last for a lot longer. To make a positive first impression, focus on the social cues you are sending out and maintain these positive signals throughout the conversation. Keep your hands visible and a genuine smile on your face.

Avoid slang and some of the typical conversation starters that are stale and lead to one-word answers. Also, steer well clear of any subjects that could be offensive and maintain a balance between listening and speaking as well as asking questions and giving your opinions.

People will often forget what you said and even how you said it. But they don't forget how you made them feel!

Conversation starters are only the beginning. As implied, it's only the first step in learning how to start a conversation. Conversations need to be maintained and even well exited. For this, it is now time for our conversation master class.

CHAPTER SIX: THE CONVERSATION MASTERCLASS

"We owe to one another all the wit and good humour we can command; and nothing so clears our mental vistas as sympathetic and intelligent conversation."

— AGNES REPPLIER

Regardless of your level of confidence, at some point in a conversation, we all think about the impression we make. We want others to see our kindness and our intelligence. Starting a conversation and actively listening won't get you to the stage where people view you the way you want them to. For this, the conversation has to keep going.

The goal of successful conversations is to find mutual interests to discover your common ground. Equally important is for your conversations to have an intention. The intention can be anything from receiving instructions to finding out more about someone to strike up a friendship. When the intention is clear, you can remove those awkward moments.

The Art of Carrying Out and Maintaining a Conversation

Everything you have learned so far is going to take you steps closer to being the master of conversations.

Let's dive straight into a step-by-step guide to having a formidable conversation before specific situations.

Step 1: Find your intention

It sounds stupid to prepare for something that should be so natural, but there are very few things we do in life without preparation, and conversations are included. Before your conversation, think of the who, the what, the when, and the why to help you identify the purpose.

Step 2: Remember the lesson on first impressions

Before you approach anything, give yourself a mental body scan to check that your body language and social cues are those you would see in a friend rather than an enemy.

Step 3: Have your conversation starters in mind

Choose three or four of the conversation starters from the previous chapter. Try to make sure they are quite different so you can start various conversations but be confident in your choice so you don't start with too many potential starters that could fluster you.

Step 4: Bookmark during conversations

Bookmarking is a way of adding emphasis to a particular part of a conversation so that it is easier to talk about it at another date. Somebody might mention something you have in common; you can comment on this and remember to talk about it again later to deepen the conversation. You may also have a shared event in the future. Others use inside jokes but take care with this in case you overuse the joke and offend others.

Step 5: Look out for sparks

Sparks are those small bursts of excitement you can see in others. It could be a smile, a twinkle in the eye, or a high tone of voice. These signs are caused by a release of dopamine, and the topic they were talking about has caused a spark in them. Use the sparks to ask more questions.

Step 6: Have some stories ready

A captivating story can have your audience on the edge of their seats. It's a chance for you to show off your wit and intelligence. You can find inspiring stories from podcasts, social media, or funny stories that have happened to other people.

Keep stories short so you don't come across as a conversation narcissist. Like conversation starters, have a few engaging stories prepared.

Step 7: Encourage their participation

Although a lot is going on, don't forget to ask some questions so you don't hog the conversation. The magic words to encourage participation are: "What's your opinion on . . .?" Be sure to check that your body language matches your genuine interest in their response.

Step 8: Know how to exit a conversation

Bookmarks are good ways to end a conversation, but as this step is so significant, we will go into more detail in a bit. For now, remember that bookmarks make a good exit strategy.

Step 9: Self-evaluation

Take a few minutes to replay the conversation to assess what went well and what signs and cues may have thrown you off. Make a point of writing down who you should follow up with and commit to doing it.

Striving for Conversation Balance

There is a lot of talk about balance in communication, the right balance of eye contact, and the right balance of speaking and listening. Within the conversation cycle, there is also a balance, and to create this, we can follow four stages.

Stage one is to inform. We enter a conversation and provide some information that opens the way to the second stage. Next, we invite the person into the conversation by asking a question. During the response, you move into stage three and listen. And the fourth stage is to acknowledge what you have heard.

To keep this cycle going, be sure to express your initial ideas clearly and with confidence. While you should always ask for clarification, if it's not needed, it is easier to flow to the following stages.

Another way to keep the cycle going is to hold back on too much detail straight away. Imagine it like a presentation at university or work. First, you would start with your bullet points to capture interest and then expand.

As you are progressing through the stages and the cycle continues, you have the opportunity to pick up on their conversation styles, what their body language is telling you, and if any cultural differences could impact the following stages, like longer pauses before speaking.

The beauty of these stages to a balanced conversation is that it is a simplistic approach but highly effective. As we move on to look at tips to keep a conversation going, think of how you can implement each stage.

• Question without interrogating: Open-ended questions provide the other person with the opportunity for an extended response and balance. Don't forget follow-up questions. For example, "What did you do at work today?"

• Visualize the other person's timeline: This is a great tip to organize your thoughts and come up with questions. Imagine the other person's timeline, some information you have. Now you need to ask questions to fill in the blanks. For example, "What are you planning to do in the holidays?"

• Avoid rows of questions: Keep in mind the cycle. In between questions, there should be responses, opinions, and follow-ups. Questions and sharing!

• Pay attention to nonverbal cues to show your interest: When you can show genuine interest, people are more likely to share information with you and ask you questions.

• Share to discover common interests: Let people know if you have read an amazing book, seen a good movie, tried a new restaurant, or anything else that really caught your interest. Share this and then ask a follow-up question to see if they share your enthusiasm.

• Face the person: If you are in a group, be sure to face the person who is talking, make eye contact with them and provide them with feedback.

• Don't come on too strong: A friendship won't naturally develop during the first conversation. Too many questions and too much enthusiasm might come across as needy and reduce the chance of further conversations.

• Conversations don't have to be linear: If you feel you are running out of conversation, know that it's okay to go back to a previous topic and go a little deeper.

• Be informed: Scan the headlines, see what's trending, and have a quick scroll through social media. It only takes a few minutes a day, but it will prepare you for relevant conversations.

• Speak your mind: Sometimes, we overthink all aspects of a conversation. For a natural approach, once in a while, just say what is on your mind—unless it's offensive. Try to stop filtering what you want to say.

- Be a novice: When we ask about people's interests, rarely do we consider what that involves and the skills that it takes. As a novice, ask questions to learn more.

- Thread your conversations: If someone mentions that they have just been on holiday or away on business, create threads on related topics. You can talk about the country or place, travel, what they had to do for work, and so on.

- Remember the Pratfall Effect: People like you more when you aren't perfect. It's okay to make mistakes and not know everything. When you allow people to see that you are a normal, fallible human, they will find it easier to relate to you.

- Don't get stuck in your own head: Remember that people you talk to are also worried about their own impressions and the stupid things they might say. Take a breath and enjoy the experience!

The smartest thing you can do to keep a conversation going is to create a safe environment for those around you. When people enter a new environment and talk to different people, they are on high alert, using their senses to assess the room.

For each new conversation, the same thing will happen. They will subconsciously scan the person to decide if there is any danger. Remember that this danger doesn't have to be physical. They, too, could fear making a fool out of themselves.

Open body language, active listening, and that all-important smile with eye contact will let them know you are no threat. This is when conversations begin to flow with ease and meaning.

We are going to take this a little further in the next section by looking at some specific situations that may require extra support.

Conversation Flow in Various Situations

Three particular areas where conversations might not flow as expected are in the workplace or at university, online, and with shy people. Let's take a look at each in more detail.

The workplace/university

The first of our potentially difficult situations is at work. While you can choose your social group, this isn't always the case when in the office, at networking events, and to an extent, at university. There will be people that you need to communicate with and, as we have learned, it is better for our mental health if you can converse with people—even those we are almost forced to connect with.

Although this has been mentioned before, it's probably more important to avoid gossip in the workplace. Some people fall into the trap of talking about others as a way to create a connection, but it's more likely that the person you are talking to loses respect. It will certainly not establish trust!

Complaining in conversations is also frowned upon and can quickly lead to gossip. At some point, there will be a need to complain about the environment where you spend most of your day. But, it should be done in a professional manner and one where the intention is to resolve the problem.

If you need to have a conversation with a coworker or even a manager, have a plan! Define the problem and be sure to have some potential solutions to offer. This way, you will come across as a problem solver rather than a complainer.

This leads nicely to the timing of your conversations. If you have ever tried to start a conversation and the other person has brushed you off, it can be upsetting and knock your confidence. It may feel like the person doesn't like you when, in fact, it is more likely that they are busy. It's a good idea to start a conversation by asking if they have a minute free and, if not, schedule a time when they do.

To be seen as a master of conversations and communication, you should be the diffuser of tension in the office. Tension leads to arguments, and if emotions aren't kept in check, feelings get unnecessarily hurt.

Two key ways to prevent arguments are by learning when to apologize and by sharing the credit. A sincere apology shows that you have the ability to recognize your mistakes and take the steps to right a wrong. It doesn't come with excuses or attempts to blame others.

At the same time, don't apologize for things that aren't your fault, even if you are desperate to ease the tension. This could be interpreted as a lack of confidence.

Just as you should be able to apologize for mistakes, you should also be able to accept compliments for work well done. Before soaking up the limelight, consider if there were other people in the process that helped you get there and give them their share of the credit.

The language you use in the workplace will differ from other social situations. While it might not be necessary to use formal language, it is crucial to remain diplomatic. You also need to ensure that both verbal and nonverbal communication is respectful. Finally, just check your language is suitable for the audience. Using complex grammatical structures and unfamiliar vocabulary can confuse your audience. You may even come across as showing off.

Online

First of all, let's get this ghosting topic out of the way! I'm not sure when this became acceptable social behavior. Not only is it unnecessary, but it is also cruel. If you aren't interested in keeping up a conversation with someone online, be honest. You might think that this will hurt them, but it won't hurt as much as them spending days and weeks wondering what happened!

For those conversations that seem to be drying up online, you can use other techniques like revisiting topics and taking them to the next level or threading into different but related topics.

The great thing about technology today is that we can instantly share so much. Just by sending a photo or a song, you have opened the path to new conversations. Imagine sending someone a song, and they had heard it at a party; you have an endless number of new questions about the event.

There are a surprising number of online activities you can also take advantage of. Imagine taking a personality quiz together. The questions that come up can lead to deeper conversations but in a less probing way. A bonus tip is to keep a note of things that pop up to discuss after the quiz too.

You can also try interactive games. One family Christmas Zoom, I remember playing online Pictionary which was hilarious and sparked some interesting conversations.

If you are struggling to read the nonverbal cues, which is only natural, don't hold back on emojis and GIFS. If you feel you are having difficulties understanding the full message, suggest a video call. This is especially useful when you first meet someone online and have never seen them face-to-face. If you notice that it's the other person struggling, suggest a call. It might be all they need to feel less insecure.

Introverts and shy people

It's particularly hard if you are both feeling the same way, but if nobody takes the first step, two introverts could end up spending more time looking at their feet than talking.

When possible, choose a location that you are both comfortable in. You will both be more at ease in a quieter coffee house than you would in a crowded bar. If it's not possible, scan the room for a more suitable area.

It's important to let introverts and shy people know that they are accepted for who they are and that nobody is trying to change them. Try to begin with a comment that will make them feel appreciated. You could thank them for agreeing to meet you at a particular place and say it meant a lot to you.

It's nice to use a mixture of open-ended questions and short answers. It can take the pressure off those longer answers where they could feel like they are being put on the spot. Another great tip is to have conversations while you are doing other activities like going for a walk or cooking.

After conversations, follow up with online communication. Introverts and shy people tend to excel at written communication. A text or email gives both of you a chance to continue conversations, strengthen the relationship, and make the next face-to-face conversation less overwhelming.

In all of the above situations, there is a risk of those awkward moments in a conversation. We will briefly look at what you can do to stop feeling awkward next.

Keeping Awkwardness at Bay

When you are unsure of social interactions and find it hard to relax around new people, you may come across as awkward. A certain amount of worry in new settings is normal, but when this stops you from doing the things you want, awkwardness is a problem.

Awkwardness doesn't just represent as difficulty in conversing. Some people feel so awkward that they end up talking too much or are excessively energetic when the mood in the room is calm.

Stop beating yourself up about your awkward moments and challenge your negative self-talk. Yes, maybe you blush every time someone asks you a question. It's not a reason for others to question your likeability or trustworthiness.

Remember that people value authenticity over someone trying to pretend they are someone they aren't.

That being said, there are still ways to keep this awkwardness at bay!

• Prepare your universal questions: Have some questions prepared that are good for any situation and any conversation. These include things like "What brings you here?" "How do you know . . .?" and "Where are you from?"

• Avoid those awkward topics: Nothing can make a conversation awkward like topics on religion, abortion, politics, and economics. I would also tread carefully when it comes to popular movements. #Me Too and #Black Lives Matter are significant but could be awkward if you don't know your audience.

• Counteract silences: When that person does start talking about tax cuts and interest rates, know how to make it more interesting. Ask what they would do with a million dollars to avoid the silence caused by boring topics.

• Take care of how much you share: A stranger once told me her 2-year-old son was a psychopath who wanted to hurt her with a knife. Awkward, and where do you take the conversation after that?

• Ask yourself what a confident person would do: Even visualize yourself as a confident person you know and think about how they would handle this situation. Would they crack a joke, tell a story, or change the subject?

• Be kind to yourself: You wouldn't tell your friend off for feeling awkward. You would support them and reassure them. Treat yourself the same way.

• Excuse yourself for a moment: If your awkwardness is so overwhelming, step away! Go to the bathroom, take deep breaths, and try a power pose or relaxation technique.

Awkwardness on the phone is a challenge because you can't read the other person and vice versa. This is especially true when it comes to time management.

Face-to-face, we can give cues to let a person know we are short of time. On the phone, we can't. Know how long your conversation should take based on the intention and begin the conversation with the expected duration.

We have seen that interrupting is a big no-no, but when it comes to phone calls, it might be necessary. When a person doesn't stop talking, be prepared to apologize for interrupting and bring them back to the topic at hand.

Don't multitask when you are on the phone. It's not something we would do in a face-to-face conversation but for some reason, it seems acceptable when on the phone.

The other person will likely pick up on your lack of attention, and even more awkward is when you respond inappropriately because you weren't actively listening.

There will also come a point where you will need to be prepared to have awkward conversations. Follow these tips to reduce the awkwardness as much as possible!

• Plan: Awkward conversations shouldn't be longer than they need to be. Know what needs to be said and stay on topic. While planning, consider your tone, body language, and other nonverbal cues.

• Choose a private place: In the middle of the workspace is obviously inappropriate but avoid any areas where others could pass. You don't need potential gossipers listening in.

• Don't allow for silence: In this situation, silence can increase a person's anxiety levels, both yours and theirs.

• Skip small talk: There is an elephant in the room, and small talk will further increase the anxiety. Get straight to the point.

• Sit down when possible: Sitting down can make people feel more comfortable. At the very least, you should make sure you are either both sitting or standing.

• Warn the person: To show empathy, let the person know that what you are about to tell them might be difficult to hear. This gives them a chance to emotionally prepare. At the same time, you can express your discomfort at having to bring up the topic.

• Give the person a chance to speak: Practice your active listening skills. Don't jump in and offer advice until you have heard all the information.

- End the conversation without awkwardness: Something simple like "Have a think about it and get back to me if you need me" shows the other person that the conversation is over in a polite way.

Speaking of awkwardness, nothing can ruin a perfect conversation quicker than an ungraceful exit. If the song "Should I Stay or Should I Go" now plays in your head, you need the final section of this chapter.

How to Graciously and Gracefully End a Conversation

As the saying goes, a bad dessert can ruin the meal! Ending a conversation the right way is going to increase the rapport you build with the person. It will leave both of you with positive emotions and create a long-lasting positive impression.

The trick is to recognize the signs of a dwindling conversation so you can end it before the awkwardness kicks in.

The first and most obvious sign is that you feel bored or like there has been a bit of an information (or emotion) overload, and you need a break. They might be feeling the same, so look out for cues like a wandering gaze, looking at their watch, fidgeting, or worse, yawning and looking for an escape route.

Sometimes, when you run out of things to say, you will notice yourself repeating things. This doesn't mean you have failed at maintaining a good conversation. All conversations have to come to an end at some point! Again, if they are repeating themselves, it's a sign to end the interaction gracefully.

As with previous subjects, we will begin with general ways to end a conversation before looking at more specific situations.

- Mention future plans: "Have a great time at . . ."

- Make a plan: "How about we grab a coffee one day to talk about this more?"

- Preempt your exit: "One more thing before I go . . ."

- Preempt your time: "I have to go in a few minutes, but I would love to hear one more joke."

- Find the host: "I haven't said hello to the host yet. Please excuse me."

- Revisit their story: "Thanks for sharing that story. It's been great talking to you."

- Rephrase their last sentence: "Your aunt isn't well. I'm so sorry to hear that. I have to run now, but I hope she gets better soon."

- Catch up with someone else: "It's been really nice talking to you, but I must catch up with my friend for a minute."

- Mention an acquaintance: "I have to go, but Jim says hi!"

- Let them finish their task: "Great to see you, but I will leave you to your walk now."

- Shake hands using the past tense: "It was lovely to meet you."

- Use your environment: "I've just seen they are serving the food. We will catch up later, okay?"

- Sit down: "As much as I have loved talking to you, I'm exhausted and need to grab a seat."

- Keep it simple: "Thanks for the chat, I have to go now" or "Please excuse me, I have to . . ."

Ending your networking conversations

- The business card collector: "So great to meet you, but I'm on a mission to collect more business cards than my last event."

- The business card giver: "Here is my card so we can discuss this more at a later date." (Alternatively, you can ask for their card.)

- Follow their promotion: "It's been really insightful; I will be sure to find out more on your website."

- Ask where something is: "Sorry, but do you know where the bathroom is?"

- Introduce them to others: "Let me introduce you to Paula. She is also rebranding at the moment."

- Ask them for introductions: "Do you know anyone else who is a developer?"

- Respect their time: "I know you have lots of other people you need to talk to. I will leave you to it."

Tying up work conversations

- There is work to be done: "It was nice talking, but I really have to catch up on my day."

- They have work to do: "Wow, you must be short of time. We can catch up later."

- Emails and calls to make: "Thanks for the chat, but I really need to send some emails."

- Have lunch: "I'm short of time now, but why don't we grab lunch?"

- Stick to the agenda: "We have covered everything on the agenda, so that's it for today."

- Let them know you will find answers: "Right now, I'm not sure, but I will let you know this afternoon."

- End Zoom fatigue: "We have gone through plenty today. We can discuss the rest in our next call."

Ending a conversation in emergency situations

You have been polite and have dropped all the nonverbal cues, but no message was received. You have combined this with verbal messages, and still, no sign that the rude, obnoxious, or narcissistic person won't give up. You are under no obligation to remain in these conversations.

→ Clap your hands: When a person refuses to stop talking, a firm clap can stop them, giving you a chance to more directly let them know it is your turn to talk.

→ Raise your hand: A stop sign with your hand can signal to someone that they have gone too far without having to verbally express your feelings.

➜ Use polite phrases to express your frustration:

"We will agree to disagree, and on that note, I must leave."

"I'm sorry I can't see your point of view but, fortunately, we are all entitled to our own opinions. Good luck."

"Our conversation was interesting. I'm going to remember you!"

In whatever way you decide to end a conversation, remember to do so politely. This means you choose a moment in the cycle where it's your turn to talk so you don't interrupt (unless forced to).

Make sure your nonverbal cues match your verbal message to leave. Start packing things up and putting things in a bag. Move to the edge of your seat so that you are signaling your exit. Sitting back and crossing your legs sends mixed signals.

And sometimes, the politest way to end a conversation is with an apology. Combining expressions like "It was so good to run into you" with "but I'm sorry, I have to go now" leaves a person feeling really good about themselves and respected.

There is one major element in conversations, however, that works like a double-edged sword.

Wield it right, and you'll be surprised how easy it becomes to have light, meaningful conversations. But if things go wrong, it can easily become extremely awkward.

You guessed it right; it's time to look at the infamous small talk.

CHAPTER SEVEN: LOVE IT? HATE IT? YOU REALLY NEED IT – SMALL TALK 101

"Normally, small talk is enough for me to form an opinion of someone. I make a quick judgment, often completely wrong, and then stick by them rigidly."

— ALEX GARLAND

There are very mixed feelings about small talk among professionals and nonprofessionals. For some, it's dull, and they would rather get straight into deeper conversations to build meaningful relationships. For others, this moment of light chit-chat can help ease tension.

But for the majority, like Alex Garland, small talk can be part of first impressions with strangers as well as other people.

While discussing the weather and sports, people are continuing to form long-lasting opinions. For this reason, small talk can't be ignored!

Small Talk – Love It or Hate It, It's Vital for Conversations Too

Small talk is defined as light and informal conversation and is most frequently used with people we don't know very well or with people we haven't seen for a while. Ironically, small talk is anything but small. During this time, our brain is processing tons of information, and a lot of that information is nonverbal. This goes for both the listener and the speaker!

Small talk provides us with a chance to find common ground and shared interests. It gives us the chance to practice our active listening skills. It's with small talk that we can overcome any anxiety the situation may have created while setting the conversation up for topics that require both parties to feel safer.

These conversations that seem unimportant give us the opportunity to show our politeness, kindness, our empathy, and even our intelligence.

Research has shown that small talk can create positive feelings and a sense of belonging (Sandstrom & Dunn, 2014). An act as simple as treating a barista the same way you would an acquaintance are important social interactions that lead to happiness.

The strategies for making small talk are the same as those we need to work on for our conversation starters. Let's take a moment to remember these crucial techniques:

- Ask open-ended questions: Think of the different responses you could get from "It's chucking it down, isn't it?" or "How do you like this weather today?"

- Actively listen: Although the response might not be the most captivating, it still requires active listening to prevent inappropriate responses and a conversation killer.

- Remove the distractions: Getting out your phone is still rude, even when it's small talk.

- Be enthusiastic: There is still fun to be had with small talk, and if you begin with a positive attitude, you are more likely to have enjoyable outcomes.

- Make the person feel comfortable: Small talk may not have a purpose like conversations do, but you can still have the intention to walk away, making the other person feel better about themselves.

You will notice some correlation between small talk and conversation starters. The main differences between small talk and conversation are the level of interest and the depth of the response. Small talk might ask someone if they got stuck in the same traffic as you did. A conversation starter would delve into how people kill time when they are stuck in traffic.

Some of the safest small talk topics include:

- The location

- Entertainment

- Art

- Food or cooking

- Hobbies

- Careers

- Sports

- The weather

- Travel

- Local attractions

As the weather is such a popular small-talk topic, we will take a moment to explore this subject more. The most typical small talk starts with something along the lines of "Gosh, it's hot today" or "It's raining cats and dogs." Because small talk is considered polite, the other person may come back with a comment about leaving their washing out and the drama this has caused.

In a brief meeting, for example, paying for something or waiting to catch public transport, a simple comment like "I hope your washing has survived the rain" has a lasting impression. You are a stranger, but you have shown genuine concern. Your small talk has just left that person with a smile on their face. It might not sound like much but put yourself in their shoes!

Now, if this was a social event and the same rain topic came up, we could turn this into a conversation starter. Here are some examples of how you can start a conversation from weather small talk:

- The possibility of a storm to clear the air, how much you hate/love storms, the last storm you had and any damage there was, a story or memory from the last storm.

- The weather and your upcoming holiday plans.

- What you love to do during the different seasons.

- Your garden, the food you are trying to grow, and how the rain helps.

- Your child who loves the rain because of the puddles they can jump in.

- How much energy you have when the sun is out and the positive mood it puts you in.

- The amazing double rainbow you saw last time it rained.

- An outdoor event you recently went to and were fortunate/unfortunate with the weather.

Notice how each thread from the weather small talk allows for the conversation cycle where both people can question and listen and experience balance between experience and ideas.

Developing and Perfecting Small Talk

Just because it's small talk, it doesn't mean to say we can't prepare for it. From the topics above, choose three or four and come up with some questions. Small talk often starts with a statement which is fine but starting with a question will lead to more potential.

The potential conflicting topics should also still be avoided. Take, for example, the topic of sports. Opening small talk with "Did you catch the game last night?" or "What an amazing game last weekend!" begins the topic but without the risk of heated opinions compared with "Didn't the Packers nail that last game?"

One of three things may happen. They may not be interested in football, in which case you can ask if they are interested in any sports. They could reply with how well the Packers played, and you have discovered common ground. Or, you will see their dislike for the Packers, and you know to tread carefully or change the subject.

Small talk isn't necessarily a time for sharing too much personal detail but sharing just the right amount can establish a greater rapport, or for brief encounters, it can put the other person at ease.

At the same time, if you know personal details about them, to create empathy, this is the time to use it. If they have children, show interest in them. If you have seen them walking their dog, ask questions. These are safe topics that help the other person feel more comfortable.

Don't take it personally if someone forgets your name. It's widely agreed that most of us are terrible with names, especially compared to remembering faces. With so many nonverbal cues flying around, you can quickly forget a name.

Rather than embarrassingly having to ask 10 minutes later, take a moment to apologize, let them know you are terrible at names, and ask them for theirs again. Not surprisingly, you may find common ground here.

Finally, imagine the person you are chatting to as a friend and not a stranger or someone you hardly know. This will help you relax, and your body will send out positive cues. In return, they will feel more relaxed, and the conversation can progress more naturally.

Small Talk for Introverts

For introverts, small talk can be painstaking and awkward, but you may find that the lead-up is what you may dread more than the small talk itself, especially when you follow the following tips:

• Lower your anxiety levels: Before approaching people or putting yourself in a situation where small talk may occur, use breathing and grounding techniques to manage your anxiety. Remind yourself that the anxiety comes from you and not the situation.

• Use positive affirmations: Replace negative assumptions with positive affirmations. For example, "Small talk has a purpose, it's fun, and I'm good at it." This is probably closer to the truth than telling yourself this is going to be awful.

• Use curiosity to your advantage: Because introverts like to discover more of the details, use small talk to uncover what would normally be skipped over.

• Add hooks to "boring" responses: Spice up your response to "How are you?" with a hook that can lead to small talk. This could be "I'm great, getting ready for my holiday" or "I'm much better now that it's time to relax."

• Be careful not to misread cues: Introverts may show cues that can be misread, whether that's you or others. Fidgeting isn't necessarily a sign of boredom, and it's more likely they are nervous. Holding back isn't because they feel they are better than you; they are just more reserved.

- Practice self-empathy: Introverts are great at concentrating for a long time, but this can backfire when it's on their own perceived faults. Try not to focus on what goes wrong but also on what you do well and praise yourself for this.

For introverts, extroverts, and all those in between, to get good at small talk, you need to commit to practicing as much as you can. Initially, the idea of striking up a conversation with someone as you wait for a bus would be terrifying. Turn your attention to making the other person feel good rather than on your nerves!

Making Small Talk More Authentic

A great place to start is to analyze the body language to decide if the other person actually wants to make small talk. Cues like feet pointing toward you, an open stance, and raised eyebrows indicate a person is interested in talking. With these signs, it's safer to say that even the small talk will be more authentic.

To be authentic, you need to show a genuine interest. Aside from active listening and working on that communication balance, it's important not to dismiss what other people are saying. This applies verbally and nonverbally. Nonverbal signs of dismissal can include scoffs or a backhanded wave. Genuine interest includes an interest in all opinions, even if you don't agree with them.

This is also true of making assumptions about other people's lives. Small talk can quickly turn into attempts of one-upping. "I'm ok, but a little tired" can lead to the other person saying, "Tell me about it, I'm exhausted because . .

." Small talk doesn't feel meaningful when everything feels like a competition.

Finally, don't forget that small talk requires good manners, encouragement through filler words and nonverbal cues, and some paraphrasing to confirm your interest and enthusiasm.

What to Do When You Really Hate Small Talk

Some may argue that you can simply avoid small talk, but this takes on a very fixed mindset where you won't be able to grow and improve yourself. At the end of the day, small talk is everywhere! If you really hate small talk, you may need to bear some of these pointers in mind in order to make it feel purposeful.

Small talk enables you to:

• Restart a paused conversation.

• Socialize with people you don't have much to say to.

• Be sociable without further expectations.

• Have social interactions when you are short of time.

• Enjoy a moment talking about the lighter things in life.

• Practice reading reading nonverbal cues and recalling information.

Another way to overcome your hatred for small talk is to see it as a goal. Set yourself a goal of starting small talk with one complete stranger that day. All goal setting requires a plan broken down into smaller steps and, of course, a reward. By rewarding yourself, your brain is more motivated to set the next small talk goal.

Visualize small talk as a bridge to deeper conversations. If you want to get to the juicy stuff, it's important to show genuine enthusiasm during the small talk stage.

We will finish off this chapter with some ways to start small talk without feeling dorky, stressed, or overwhelmed.

Questions to Take the Awkwardness Out of Small Talk

Below you will find a list of 26 small talk questions you can use in a wide range of situations. Instead of just remembering a few, let's work a little harder to prepare ourselves for the next moment we need to practice small talk.

For each of the following phrases, consider the situation you would use them in, the level of closeness to the person (complete stranger or friend), and what follow-up questions you could ask to turn the small talk into a conversation. Even think if there are alternatives that you could add to your collection.

1. How did you get this role?

2. What's up with this weather today?

3. How long have you been in this department?

4. How long have you been waiting for . . .?

5. What was your first job?

6. What was the last podcast you listened to?

7. What pets do you have?

8. If you could have any pet, what would it be?

9. Of all your hobbies, which do you prefer the most?

10. Who is your favorite actor?

11. Have you worked remotely before?

12. Are there any cheap places to eat around here?

13. Would you rather cook or be cooked for?

14. Where did you go on your last holiday?

15. Are you planning any trips soon?

16. What was your favorite subject in school?

17. If you could teach, what subject would it be?

18. What type of car do you drive?

19. What is the one food you would never eat?

20. What movie do you hate that everyone else loves?

21. What is the highlight of your day so far?

22. What are your plans for this evening?

23. When was the last time you moved house?

24. Have you heard this speaker before?

25. Do you know of any good gyms around here?

26. Did you catch the news today?

We will finish off this chapter with two examples of small talk that tick all the boxes using our friends Emily and Sophie again. In the first case, Emily is working in a grocery store at the checkout. They know each other by sight but have never had a conversation.

- Emily: "Hello!"

- Sophie: "Hello! I love what you have done with your hair today."

- Emily: "Thank you, the kids woke me up too early, so I had time to actually do my hair."

- Sophie: "It's a luxury when you get a few minutes to yourself, isn't it? How old are they?"

- Emily: "Seven and five. Do you have kids?"

- Sophie: "Yes, They are eight and four. I have to rush and pick them up now"

- Emily: "What school do they go to?"

- Sophie: "St. James's, so at least it's not far."

- Emily: "Oh, mine too. Maybe I will see you at the gate. I hope you make it on time."

- Sophie: "Thanks. See you soon and good luck getting another 5 minutes of peace today!"

Fortunately, a few weeks later, Emily and Sophie are waiting at the school gates, and their small talk has the opportunity to turn into a more interesting conversation. Sophie has made an effort to recall information before starting the small talk, which will instantly put Emily at ease.

- Sophie: "Hi! Did you get your extra 5 minutes this morning or not so lucky?"

- Emily: "Hi! (Smiling.) Yes, I did, but I chose to enjoy a quiet coffee instead. How is your day going so far?"

- Sophie: "Productive. I still have after-school activities, but I will take the chance to catch up on some emails."

- Emily: "My youngest does rhythmic gymnastics, and it's adorable to watch. But there is only so much spinning you can watch for an hour! What are yours into?"

- Sophie: "Ivan loves football, and Sam is really into Zumba. If they had it their way, they would be doing something every day, but with their homework, I think it's too much. There aren't enough hours in the day."

- Emily: "I know. I actually go to Zumba once a week, and I feel guilty that I'm not at home with them."

- Sophie: "No way! You do Zumba? I started last year at the gym in town, but I didn't like the instructor."

- Emily: "I've heard the same from others. I go to the class on Thursdays in the mall. You should sign up!"

- Sophie: "I might do that. Next time I see you, I will grab the number. Thanks. You have made my day!"

- Emily: "My pleasure. We could go all out and get a drink after!

Notice how in both cases, the women share enough information that is comfortable. They are honest and empathetic without trying to start some weird mom competition. At the end of each conversation, they have made sure to end on a high so that the next interaction is easier to start, and they can both walk away with a positive impression.

One of the key things that helped turn their small talk into a conversation was that neither of them fell into the phenomenon of 'mirroring.' This is when one person says something, and the other person pretty much repeats it.

When Sophie said there were not enough hours in the day, Emily could have mirrored, "No, there aren't enough hours in the day!" and the conversation may have come to a lull or an awkward silence.

So, despite small talk having a bit of a boring, negative reputation, it certainly doesn't have to be this way. On the contrary, when you adjust your frame of mind and appreciate small talk for its benefits, you will find you can get a lot out of it, not just when it comes to building and strengthening relationships but for your mental health too.

Small talk and conversations is one thing but thinking in a clear way and not letting emotions come in between is another. Let's see how you can stop overthinking when engaged in conversations with others.

CHAPTER EIGHT: ORDER FROM CHAOS

"Chaos was the law of nature; Order was the dream of man."

— HENRY ADAMS

Years ago, when I was developing my conversational skills, my mind was in absolute chaos. I took on too much learning at once. And when this was mixed in with my anxiety and how I was feeling about different situations and conversations, it is safe to say my biggest dream was some order in my life!

The Next Set of Complications That Hinder Effective Communication

Both our verbal and nonverbal communication can be distorted by our intrapersonal and interpersonal conditions as well as the environment we are in. The environment can be easier to understand. If you are in a dark alley, both you and the other person are going to be more alert, perhaps even more suspicious of everything that is going on. Let's briefly consider other factors that can impact our communication:

• Preoccupation: People worry, often about the impression they make, that they don't take in the full message.

• Emotional blockages: The conversation is so charged with messages that it affects how the message is expressed and interpreted.

• Hostility: Anger in the moment or from a previous conversation, and the conversation is fueled by venting.

• Charisma: Someone delivering a message in such a charismatic way can distort the message because by making something grander than it may be, the listener is less likely to question what is being said.

• Past experiences: We might be inclined not to actively listen based on our past experiences and bias of similar situations.

• Hidden agendas: Hidden agendas can cause both the speaker and the listener to only hear what serves their individual needs.

• Mind wandering: As we have previously seen, a wandering mind doesn't allow for active listening and might be caused by preoccupation.

• Defensiveness: When people are insecure, they can become defensive and misinterpret the message or the purpose of the message.

- Status: Those of lower status could be worried about making a good impression. Those with higher status may have to deal with envy but also the impression they make on those of all statuses.

Overcoming these factors requires thinking and feeling. You can imagine these two acts as head talk (the thinking), which explains the interactive situation, and gut talk (the feeling) and how we understand our interactions.

Our think statements are somewhat natural and involve definitions, assertions, and connections. They are statements of logic, rules, truth, or a lack of truth. They require us to use our brains. When we say, "I think this is a bad idea," it is because we are basing our phrase on logic and reason.

When we use feeling phrases, we are tuning into our gut and instincts. There can be no right or wrong or even good or bad, only honest feelings and dishonest feelings. Notice the same sentence, but from the gut, "I feel this is a bad idea." The impact of the message is not the same. Because it's not factual, it doesn't carry the same weight.

Humans are good at conditioning themselves when it comes to our internal feelings, especially when it comes to more intense emotions. This becomes a problem because it causes emotional blockages, which limit our experiences.

There are other issues when it comes to dealing with our feelings. Projection is a common problem in groups when we deny our true feelings, projecting them onto others as a way to justify a bias.

Some people fall into the trap of guessing other people's emotions and trying to determine why they feel a particular way. Essentially, this takes the focus off the message and leads to attempts of mind reading.

Metafeelings are the ultimate way to create chaos in the mind. Imagine sentences like "I guess that when I feel . . ." These metafeelings are thoughts and feelings about your feelings. Metafeelings include anxiety caused when thinking of a fear or shame as a result of sadness or disgust.

For our communication to be both effective and meaningful, we need to develop the ability to own our thoughts and feelings. Taking responsibility for the head and the gut means the other knows exactly where you stand and, therefore, where they stand. The end result is that communication is authentic!

Let's tackle our emotions first!

Keeping Your Emotions in Check

There will have been occasions when your attempts at communication have gone sideways because you thought you had your emotions under control, but your body was telling the listener something completely different. The brain was telling you to calm down and not explode in anger, but your cues were giving your true feelings away. A lot of our nonverbal cues depend on emotional regulation.

When we improve our emotional regulation, our communication gets better. This is because we are better at not only understanding our own thoughts and feelings, but the message is received more clearly because we learn to identify the emotions of others.

Emotional regulation isn't about ignoring intense feelings. They need to be processed and understood. But with so much going on in our communication, the first stage is to calm down so we can be fully present.

• Breath: It's so easy to forget to take a breath to calm your autonomic nervous system down and come out of the fight, flight, or freeze mode! Be mindful of your breath and your senses.

• Anchor your body: Touch each finger with your thumb while counting, or firmly press each toe to the ground while counting. This grounding technique can help you break out of rumination and stay focused.

• Move: Standing up or walking around helps the thinking part of our brain to activate. Be sure to do this in a nonaggressive way, so mention that you feel the need to stand up or stretch a bit.

• Listen to your body: If your heart is racing and you can feel the tension building up, it only takes a few seconds to calm down and not say something you will regret. Open your arms, pull your shoulders back, and allow your lungs to fill with oxygen. As you breathe out, visualize the tension leaving your body.

• Use a calming mantra: Have a short sentence you can repeat in your head to remind your brain you are in control. Try phrases like "I am capable of solving this problem" or "I am in control of my emotions."

- Forbid transference: If someone else is angry, sarcastic, or manipulative, don't let their issues transfer onto you. This will only spiral out of control. Again, use visualization to image a protective shield around you.

- Clarification is crucial: If we are communicating with our gut and not our mind, it's easy to misinterpret the message as emotions are blocking it. If you have any doubts, ask for more information or paraphrase what they said.

- Don't ignore your gut: Though we want to engage thinking, you are now or soon to be a master of nonverbal cues. If you sense something isn't right, have faith in your instincts.

- Take responsibility: If a mistake was made on your behalf, own it. You will gain far more respect, and the tension will dissipate. This goes for taking responsibility for your emotions too. If you feel that you have acted inappropriately, apologize.

- Empathize to an extent: Only you are responsible for your emotions and, at the same time, the other person has to be responsible for theirs. Show empathy when people are stressed and overwhelmed, but this isn't an excuse for aggressive or abusive behavior.

- Take a break: If the conversation remains emotionally charged despite your efforts, let the other person know that you are going to take a moment to think about what was said and will come back to it once you have considered everything.

- Take time to process: After a particularly emotional conversation, take a few moments to label your emotions as accurately as possible. Do the same for the other person based on their verbal and nonverbal cues. Also, consider why the emotions were present.

We need to break out of the thought that emotions are either good or bad. All emotions, especially in communication, have a purpose. When used the right way, these perceived negative emotions can help us.

For example, if you are angry and have taken the time to process it but are still angry, it's a sign that you need to talk to the person who has caused this.

While you don't want to show sadness when trying to make a positive first impression, it's okay to show your vulnerability to some people.

Anxiety is particularly harmful when bottled up. Sometimes, acknowledging and admitting your tensions is enough to make yourself feel better. On the other hand, you wouldn't want to admit anxiety when others are looking to you for confidence.

There is beauty in taking a moment to pause. Recognizing and accurately labeling emotions takes practice, and even then, sometimes, we can confuse them.

If you are unsure about your emotion and whether it could do harm or good, take a moment to pause. Like taking a deep breath, we are talking about a few seconds that could literally change the effectiveness of your communication.

So, we have mentioned that we need to regulate our emotions and encourage the thinking side of ourselves, but what happens when we think too much?

Talk, Don't Overthink

There is no doubt that technology has changed communication for the better, but if we remove the rose-tinted glasses, we can also see that it can have negative consequences—overthinking!

How often have you gone to post a message on social media and spent too much time considering your wording, then posting it only to think that you got it all wrong? How do you feel when someone reads your message and doesn't reply?

Once again, we waste time overthinking what is wrong, possibly even sending another message asking why the person is mad at us. In all that overthinking, we don't consider that maybe they are just busy!

Overthinking is a form of self-torture that only creates more problems to deal with. Whether face-to-face or digitally, when we get stuck in our own minds, we aren't listening or talking!

In this section, we are going to take a closer look at how we can stop overthinking in order to improve communication.

• Recognize overthinking: Because it's a cycle, overthinking won't just top unless you make it. It's important to know when your thoughts aren't serving a useful purpose and address it. Tell yourself, "I'm overthinking, and it's time to stop."

• Look for evidence: Engage in your thinking side and discover if there is any truth to what is causing your rumination. Be careful not to get caught up in cognitive distortions such as catastrophizing or fortune-telling.

• Put things in perspective: Is this a life or death situation? By overthinking, are you going to solve a problem, or are you procrastinating?

• Accept what is in your control: If your overthinking is about something you can't control, you are likely to just cause yourself more stress and anxiety, and the cycle continues.

• Redirect your energy: If you are in a face-to-face conversation, pull your attention to their body language, specifically the microexpressions that require more effort to read. If it's digital, walk away and do something different to break the cycle.

• Try not to take things personally: As you have discovered, communication is a complex process, and not everyone gets it right all the time. If someone behaves in a strange way, remind yourself that it is probably not because of you.

• Practice mindfulness: Mindfulness engages the senses and encourages us to slow down both physically and mentally. Breathwork and guided meditation are two ways to become more mindful and enjoy the present.

• Find your 'can-do' attitude: Overthinking the problem delays taking action. Break your problem down into smaller steps and jump straight into the first step. You will find your momentum!

• Try an improv class: It might sound a bit extreme, but improv classes involve role-playing and spontaneity, and there is no room for overthinking. It's also a chance to see that things don't always go to plan, but it's not the end of the world.

• Make mistakes on purpose: Another one that sounds extreme but it can help to make mistakes intentionally. If you are overthinking what can go wrong, deliberately making a mistake allows you to face fears, especially when it comes to other people's reactions

• Check your self-esteem: Overthinking in conversations could be a sign of low self-esteem. Remind yourself of what we learned in Chapter Two so that you are continuously working on your self-esteem and self-awareness.

Overthinking is, unfortunately, a very natural habit. It's important not to extend the cycle by thinking too much about your overthinking. These strategies will reduce overthinking in conversations, but you really shouldn't beat yourself up for it.

On the other hand, when overthinking starts to negatively impact your life, it might be time to talk about your thoughts and feelings. This could be with a friend or therapist. Overthinking is particularly destructive for those with social anxiety, introverts, and shy people.

Social anxiety, introversion, and shyness can all lead to a fear of being judged or rejected socially, which, in turn, leads to overthinking. Apart from the above techniques, it's important for you to understand your self-worth in order to stop overthinking social situations.

Validate yourself so that you don't go into social situations looking for validation from others. Write a list of everything you are good at and read the list often. Try to avoid comparing yourself to others, and this may involve a digital detox, especially from social media. And don't forget to practice self-care. Eat the right foods, get enough sleep, and exercise.

Whether it's social situations, conversations you are about to have, or conversations that have now passed, it's a good idea to set aside some time and give yourself permission to overthink. Treat it as a daily session to get it out of your system. Set a timer for 10 minutes, choose a quiet place and either think, speak out loud, or write down your ruminations. Be firm with yourself. Once the timer goes off, it's time to get on with your action plan!

Rumination and overthinking are both psychologically perplexing topics, and it's impossible to examine the topics in depth here. If you feel you need more support, understanding, and strategies, you can check out my books *How to Stop Negative Thinking* and *How to Stop Overthinking*.

Now that we understand more about overthinking, it will be easier to see why, in some conversations, we simply can't seem to stop talking!

No More Rambling – Keeping Thoughts Organized

We are all under the impression that there is a thinking process, which is true, but it gives us the idea that one step logically follows the next. We have an idea, and we blurt it out. The idea might not make sense because the thoughts are still jumbled up in our minds.

Often, this goes back to our emotions. Some people find themselves extremely nervous or excited, and they start to speak too quickly. This can confuse the listener and you can see this, so you just keep talking, hoping that the pieces of your idea will eventually make sense. You may start speaking even quicker in the hope of maintaining focus. But the opposite occurs.

First things first, remember the 5 Ps—Proper Preparation Prevents Poor Performance. Our brains need a moment, sometimes longer, to process thoughts and ideas and prepare them in a logical way. Whether you are about to give an hour-long presentation or catch up with your friends, it's necessary to think about what you say before you speak.

During this time, you can decipher what is relevant and what is not so that you can stay on topic. As well as what you are going to say, you can prepare how you are going to say it. You don't need to sound smart or overcomplicate things. You need to make sure your vocabulary, language, and tone are suitable for your audience.

Aside from your preparation, here are some more tips to prevent disorganized thoughts and rambling:

• Read as much as possible: Read newspapers, magazines, books, and blogs. All of these resources will expand your vocabulary and teach you how to express things in different ways.

• Practice expressing yourself in different ways: To maintain the attention of your audience, avoid repeating words and structures. Instead of saying thank you 10 times, try "Much appreciated," "I owe you," or "You are the best."

• Write down your learning: Writing down what you have learned turns ideas into visual sentences. Writing keeps your thought process concise while linking ideas in a structure.

• Focus on one topic: Once one topic has been completely dealt with and there are no loose ends or confusion, then it is time to move on to the next.

• Pause: Pauses in a conversation allow for many things to happen. You can breathe, your mind has a few seconds to process the next thought, and your audience has a moment to digest the message.

• Stop overthinking by focusing on others: The fastest way to jumble your thoughts is to think about them too much. Look at what others are doing as you speak so you can better engage with others rather than speed thinking!

• Stop your rambling with a question: If you find yourself talking too much, stop and ask a question. Like pauses, this gives you a moment to get back on track.

• Don't fear silence: Some people can't stop talking because they are scared that silence is a bad thing. Allow for a few seconds of silence before feeling the need to talk again.

• Get treatment for underlying issues: People with Asperger's syndrome, ADHD, and anxiety disorders may ramble as a way of avoiding internal experiences. Treating the condition can reduce rambling without having to directly work on it.

Public speaking is one of the most nerve-wracking experiences that most of us have to go through at some point. This can quickly lead to rambling not only because we are anxious but because it is harder to maintain the focus of a group compared to just one or two people.

To prevent rambling in front of your larger audience and increase engagement, you need to follow the PREP framework. PREP stands for Point, Reason, Example, and Point. Let's see it in action.

• Point: "We need to come up with ways to reduce our overheads."

• Reason: "Due to increased costs, our quarterly profits are lower, and this will impact future investments."

• Example: "If we can source alternative materials that don't reduce the quality of our product, our bottom line will increase."

• Point: "By reducing overheads, we will have the resources to invest in the new technology we have all been keen on."

Following these four simple steps leaves no room for rambling because your audience knows exactly what you are trying to say. You are on topic; it's kept short and to the point, and there is little room for misunderstandings because there is no fluff in between the steps.

It seems like quite a direct approach, even cold and rude, but it is actually just a way of being assertive. There are times when we need to drive a point home in a stronger manner. Being assertive and not rambling keeps people interested. And keeping people interested will keep them coming back to you for more!

CHAPTER NINE: THE INTEREST FACTOR

"To be yourself in a world that is constantly trying to make your something else is the greatest accomplishment."

— RALPH WALDO EMERSON

We need to be genuine and authentic, but this is often a challenge when we are self-conscious about how we come across to others.

Of course, we want to come across as kind and intelligent, but at the same time, the last thing you want to do is bore your audience.

Like communication as a whole, the interest factor is a two-way street. As much as you want the other person to be interested in you, you also need to show interest in them.

We have seen how nonverbal communication can project interest in what the other person is saying. Now it's time to learn how you can keep your conversation engaging.

Steps to Develop the Interest Factor

Small talk is the foundation of developing interesting conversations. Asking appropriate questions, such as those that comply with FORD, can prevent you from getting stuck on meaningless topics. When a conversation becomes too one-sided, someone is going to get bored. So, be sure to offer up some personal information about yourself too.

When people share information, try to keep the focus on what they are saying rather than slipping into overthinking mode. When someone talks about their last holiday, rather than thinking you know nothing about the location and therefore you will kill the conversation, ask a follow-up question.

Once you have laid the groundwork with small talk, it's time to move on to deeper conversations, and this is where our curiosity comes into play. Curiosity is like the glue that keeps our conversations going strong.

When we are curious, different parts of the brain are activated. One of these is the substantia nigra, which is responsible for producing dopamine. Another is the ventral tegmental area. This part of the brain plays a role in our motivation and cognition. Finally, the hippocampus is activated and helps with our learning and memory.

Essentially, curiosity helps with our happy hormones, the positive feelings we have about a conversation, and our ability to recall information. For this reason, by staying curious, we maintain interest. How do we do this?

• Set realistic expectations: Not everyone you meet is going to be super interesting, and your level of interest is going to depend on the relationship with the person. You will be more interested in what your friend did over the weekend than a stranger.

• Check your preconceived notions: If we have formed opinions of someone before a conversation, it might be hard to overcome them and find interest. Just because someone "looks" boring, it doesn't mean they are.

• What does interesting mean to you: Be curious about your spectrum of interests and what it takes for other people to be interesting to you. Are you more interested in a certain type of person or topic?

• Calm your inner critic: It's hard to be curious about others when you are worried about your clothes or the hairstyle that isn't quite perfect. Forgive your imperfections because you don't need more anxiety.

• Look for details: Look for the smaller details to pay compliments and spark engaging conversations. This is particularly beneficial if you spot a unique piece of jewelry or another accessory.

• Create recall flashcards: If you aren't good at remembering details, create flashcards for people, which you can revise before social events.

• Appreciate people's differences: Our social interactions are more diverse than ever, and you may feel like this creates barriers to common ground. Respectfully be curious about your differences.

- See your differences as strengths: What you may see as a flaw in yourself can be a strength to others and something they might be interested in.

- Find like-minded people: If you find it really difficult to keep your interest, start by talking to people when doing hobbies and activities you like. You already have a common interest.

- Follow your interests: Use technology to your advantage and follow groups and other people who are into the same things as you. This can be a safer environment to practice your conversation skills.

- Try new interests: When we try new things, a wave of fresh excitement is transmitted when we talk about it. Plus, you are learning more and expanding your social circles.

- Be comfortable changing the topic: If you are bored with the subject, look for a lull in the conversation, and don't be scared to change it with one of the conversation starters from Chapter Five.

- Assume you have something in common with everyone: Ask enough questions, listen, and share, and you will find something in common.

- Acknowledge points well made: People are used to conversations where someone is trying to get one up on the other person. Recognizing points well made by others is refreshing, creates balance, and helps open the conversation up to other possibilities.

- Don't be afraid to admit that you don't know: As much as you want to come across as smart, it doesn't make sense to fake your way through a conversation. Admitting you don't know is honest. Just try to add a phrase after so as not to kill the conversation.

• Ask about passions and dreams: We have moved past small talk now, and we are working on developing a closer relationship. One thing is to talk about hobbies, and another thing is to talk about what really motivates people in life.

Attention is essential for curiosity and interest. In a natural conversation, the subject will start to change, but that doesn't mean a topic has been fully covered. Make a big effort to remember details about the interests of others so that later on, you can ask open-ended questions to discover more.

That being said, there are some questions that we do want to avoid.

The Dangers of Pseudo-Questions

"If a tree falls in a forest and no one is around to hear it, does it make a sound?" This is a classic example of a pseudo-question.

Pseudo-questions are those that can't be answered or a question that is formed in a way that is only offering an opinion or statement.

This quickly takes any interest out of a conversation because the asker isn't genuinely interested in the response. But it could be a way for them to strongly encourage the other person to agree with what they are saying.

Here are the principal types of pseudo-questions:

1. Co-optive questions

These are questions where the asker is only trying to get a response they want to hear or one that suits their agenda. They could begin with things like "Don't you think . . .?" or "Wouldn't you prefer . . .?"

2. Punitive questions

By definition, punitive means punishment, so these questions aim to punish a person or expose them in some kind of way without doing it directly. It would involve asking for evidence when it isn't there. Normally, the question just puts the other person on the spot.

3. Hypothetical questions

For me, these are often a waste of time. When someone asks what I would have done differently, they are often just trying to find ways to criticize what somebody else had done. "If" and "what if" don't serve a purpose because we weren't in that situation, so we can't attest to what we would have done.

Nevertheless, there are some types of hypothetical questions that can be fun and entertaining. For example, "What would you do if you met your favorite celebrity?" or "If you won a million dollars, how would you spend it?"

4. Imperative questions

This is a classic example of a question that is really a command. When a parent asks their child if they have done their homework (knowing full well they haven't), they would ask, "Have you done your homework yet?" They aren't interested in the answer; they are using the question to indirectly tell their child to do it.

5. Screened questions

Screened questions mask what a person is too afraid to ask directly. If two people are going out for dinner, instead of asking what food they would like, they ask if the other person would like (say) Italian, hoping that this person agrees. How is this person going to react if they don't like Italian? Risk upsetting the asker or sitting through a meal they don't like?

6. Set-up questions

When a person sets another person up with questions like "Is it fair to say . . ." or "Wouldn't you agree . . .? the asker is playing on the vulnerability of others. They are being led to a particular response.

7. Rhetorical questions

A rhetorical question has many forms, but one use could be to create drama or emphasize a point instead of getting an answer. People can phrase questions to make a suggestion appear like a group one. Of course, it may also be to almost force someone into agreeing with a one-word question such as "Right? or "Okay?"

8. "Gotcha" questions

This is simply a way to try and catch someone out or trap them. They are quite often almost probing or gossipy type questions like "Didn't I see you . . .?" or "Weren't you the one who . . .?"

As you may have noticed, these questions have probably been quite common in your communication. It's okay because you aren't alone in using these indirect forms of communication. In fact, now that you are aware of them, you are likely to notice other people using them.

From your part, try to be more direct with your communication and use statements rather than trying to phrase them as a question. Don't try to hide your ideas and opinions in a question.

Let's get back to captivating our audience with the art of storytelling.

How to Tell Captivating Stories

Your introductions, small talk, and conversations are going well. You are comfortable talking about your FORD topics and divulging just enough personal information. Along with eye contact, verbal signs of interest, and a healthy balance between listening and speaking, it feels like you really have this communication under control.

Then you turn around and notice someone with a crowd around them, all fixated on this person, hanging onto every word they say. What does this person have? The ability to tell amazing stories.

Storytelling is the way we exchange information about our life experiences. When we share our stories, we get social feedback, and that feedback helps us to shape our identity.

These stories are also a way to connect and identify with others.

Stories can communicate behavior and norms, the good and the bad. Gossiping falls outside the acceptable social rules, but at the same time, retelling a story of kindness or heroism shows others important values.

When you can successfully hold the attention of a crowd, you will get a great confidence boost and a bit of a healthy ego boost. Talking about yourself activates the same part of the brain as eating good food and having sex. It feels good to talk about ourselves and to have people interested.

Follow these strategies to improve your storytelling skills!

• Choose stories that are worth telling: Take a scroll through your memories for stories that are eventful or have a particular purpose. If it's someone else's story, why did it interest you?

• Know your story genre: Stories can be amusing, scary, and sad, to name a few. Your tone has to be right for the story, and more importantly, make sure your story is appropriate for the situation.

• Hook the audience from the beginning: People's time and energy are precious, and they won't listen if they aren't interested from the beginning. Your hook also needs to be relevant to the situation.

• Build tension: After you hook the audience, it's time to build up the tension as the story progresses. This will maintain the attention to the end.

• Use your body language: Your gestures and expressions can convey emotions in the story. How you move indicates your own level of interest in the story.

• Enable the audience to empathize: Tell your story in a way that allows the audience to feel what the characters feel to draw them further into the story. This also means that your characters need to be relatable.

• Think about the level of detail: A good story has enough detail to paint an accurate picture without going over the top and making the story too long or distracting from the main point of the story. Overexplaining kills their imagination!

• Share your eye contact: If your story is being told to a group, you need to make sure you are looking at everyone. Every now and then, shift your gaze to someone different so that everyone is included.

• Pace your story: Which parts of your story are better with faster speech, and where would a pause be beneficial? Remember how these details can covey things like excitement and suspense.

• Remember your tone: Lowering your tone of voice can emphasize sadness, increasing the tone. You can revise Chapter Five for ways to use your voice more effectively.

• Know how to end your story: Whether it's a punchline or the key detail, the end of your story needs to have a lasting impact on your audience. Don't let any distractions stop you from finishing the story.

• Start with one person: Practice telling your story to one person, then two, and gradually work your way up to groups. The focus should always be on the story, not the number of people you are telling it to.

• Watch videos: Public speaking videos will help you to see how people use their communication skills to captivate the audience, but if you want to go one better, watch stand-up comedians, the masters of storytelling.

• Don't give up: It will take a few attempts to actually feel confident telling stories, especially with larger groups, but that doesn't mean to say that you aren't getting it right! Have a storytelling goal and reward yourself for your achievements.

Storytelling is a wonderful way to strengthen relationships.

It moves us past the basics of getting to know each other and reveals more about our past and how our experiences have led us to where we are today.

Just remember that although storytelling boosts our happy feelings, it's also important to respect others and pay attention to their stories.

It's highly likely that they have interesting stories that you will be able to share with others, giving you more chances to practice!

Not all stories have to be funny, but as Peggy Noonan said, "Wit is a function of verbal intelligence," and as we strive to engage in intelligent and interesting communication, wit is the key to both.

Charming Conversations – The Art of Witty Banter

Witty banter is a humorous and clever way to make conversations more interesting. Witty people are able to draw unique connections between ideas and observations. Imagine wit as verbal gymnastics, playing with words and language to build rapport, trust, and even intimacy.

Some people seem to be naturally wittier than others, but it's a skill that can be learned more easily if you keep expanding your vocabulary and linguistic knowledge.

Witty banter changes depending on the people, the situation, and different personalities. There are some bantering styles: witty flirting, mild sarcasm, self-deprecating humor, playful teasing, and goofy responses. Before looking closer at different types of banter, let's look at why it's good for us.

This type of playfulness creates closer connections in casual situations. People who are able to laugh together are able to build more trust and intimacy. At the same time, it gives you a chance to show your intelligence and knowledge without being too serious.

Knowing when and how to use wit can take all conversations to the next level. It can make a boring conversation more interesting. A well-timed pun, metaphor, or movie quote can ease the tension and clear the slate for a new conversation topic.

There are some basic what-not-to-dos when it comes to witty banter. It's crucial that you use this skill the right way.

If not, you can come across as uneducated, sarcastic, and even rude.

• Only banter with those you know: Everyone's sense of humor is different. Until you get to know a person, you won't know how they will react to your banter.

• Banter shouldn't emphasize faults: While you can joke about some things, it's never good to cause offense or make fun of people. Be aware of the line between banter and being nasty.

• Know what to avoid: Just like in conversations, there are controversial topics, including people's insecurities, which should be off limits, even if you know them well.

• Backhanded compliments aren't funny: "Your hair looks lovely today. Did you wash it?" It's supposed to be a compliment, but really, it is an insult that implies they don't wash their hair often enough.

• Know when to stop: Pay extra attention to nonverbal cues to ensure the other person isn't uncomfortable or you haven't taken things too far. If you have, an apology will go a long way.

Now on to the good stuff. Let's start with general tips and techniques to start adding witty banter to conversations.

• Confidence helps wit: If you aren't comfortable with who you are, wit won't flow naturally. Your comments need to be said loud and clear and at ease in the social situation.

• Work on your body language: There is no room for mixed messages with witty banter. If you make a playful remark, your body language can't be closed off or aggressive.

• Combine your wit with facial expressions: A subtle smile, a raised eyebrow, or biting your lip can add to the impact.

• Practice with the right people: Like your confidence, you won't feel comfortable practicing your wit with people who unsettle you. Try your witty banter out on siblings and cousins or close friends.

• Take advantage of your storytelling skills: Your own experiences are perfect for witty remarks that make the story funnier. Have a memory of a few stories and where there is room for wit.

• Get the timing right: We are all familiar with a smart comment as soon as someone walks away, but you don't want to rush it either. Interrupting is rude, while a second of pause can add to the humor.

• Find the unexpected links: Sometimes, the funniest things come about because of the element of surprise. Think *Peppa Pig* and a *Full English Breakfast!*

• Practice being goofy: Goofy sounds and facial expressions can help you to lighten up and bring out the more playful side of you. If you need goofy inspiration, watch Jim Carrey in action.

• Try self-deprecating humor: This is a safe way to practice wit because you are making fun of your own shortcomings. People who are able to crack a joke about themselves are more likely to be seen as trustworthy.

- Stay present: If you are overthinking or your mind starts to wander, you will miss out on opportunities to use your knowledge and humor!

- Watch sitcoms: There are plenty of sitcoms where one or more of the characters are naturally funny. When it comes to intelligent humor, my go-to is *Frasier* because the five main characters each have a different style.

- Bantering over text: Remember that with a lack of nonverbal cues, it's easier to take teasing and banter the wrong way. Say your text aloud and use emojis and GIFs to emphasize playfulness.

Witty banter is ideal when it comes to flirting. It can remove any initial awkwardness. Humor and intelligence are both highly desirable qualities and can increase attractiveness. In many ways, bantering with your crush is much like bantering with a friend, but you need to increase certain signals to make sure the interest is there.

First of all, long, lingering eye contact creates intimacy. A smile, a grin, or a wink, especially during a moment of silence, can fuel the spark between you. You should also add more compliments in between the teasing so they know you like them that way and in case they didn't pick up on your nonverbal cues.

Be careful not to cross the line and end up negging. This is when banter goes too far, and the other person only ends up feeling bad about themselves. Lowering a person's self-esteem in the hope of them needing your approval is emotional manipulation.

Other signs of manipulation over banter include comments that are far from honest, a lack of boundaries, and playing on your guilt. Anyone who is passive-aggressive is also misusing witty banter!

As you may not know the person as well as you do your friends, stick to very light, non-offensive teasing—especially something they have brought up about themselves. Things like being a neat freak or a terrible cook are safe.

When others are bantering with you, the best thing is to play along with their jokes. Most of the time, they are just trying to build a rapport with you rather than cause offense. It's also good practice to remember that they, too, might be learning how to develop their wit. At the same time, if someone is just being rude, you don't need to tolerate it!

Now that we have moved toward keeping things interesting in conversations, it is time to see how, outside of storytelling, you can have meaningful conversations, forge emotional connections, and make friends.

CHAPTER TEN: MEANINGFUL CONVERSATIONS AND CONNECTIONS

"Deep human connection is . . . the purpose and the result of a meaningful life – and it will inspire the most amazing acts of love, generosity, and humanity."

— MELINDA GATES

There is no need to rehash all of the negatives in the world. Instead, wouldn't it be nice if we could all experience more acts of love, generosity, and humanity? We have mentioned the importance of rapport. Once rapport is established, then we can begin to appreciate meaningful connections.

How to Build Better Rapport with People

Rapport is important for our personal and professional lives because it is how we emotionally connect with others. It's a process that can sometimes happen almost instantly and other times take a little longer.

On some occasions, we may meet people and feel there is nothing in common, and the rapport is much harder to develop. This is why small talk is so essential. With the right small talk skills, you will find it much easier to find your common ground.

Let's revise the essentials of small talk to start building rapport faster.

- Check that you are dressed appropriately for the occasion.

- Keep your body language open and friendly, gently leaning in to show interest.

- Remember the rules of conversation and the balance between listening and speaking.

- Start with safe, noncontroversial topics and ask open-ended questions to discover more.

- Add clean humor for a shared laugh and greater trust.

- Be determined to find common ground and shared experiences.

- Work on your emotional awareness so that you can respond appropriately.

- Mirror nonverbal cues.

- Show empathy and understanding.

Although we have looked at lots of questions for both small talk and conversation starts, here are eight more that will get you on your way to better rapport:

1. What's the best piece of advice you have received?

2. What achievement are you most proud of?

3. What superpower would you choose to have and why?

4. What's the most interesting thing you have learned recently?

5. What is one problem you have that you wish you could solve today?

6. Who is someone you admire or respect?

7. Which city or country do you most want to visit?

8. What's the most exciting thing that has happened to you recently?

By now, you have probably had a chance to practice your small talk, and you will have noticed how conversations with both strangers and acquaintances are getting easier and even more enjoyable. Now, it's time to start with topics that are really going to create connections.

Moving Conversations toward Deep and Meaningful

To begin, it's necessary to keep in mind that not everyone is ready for deep and meaningful conversations. They might not be in the right frame of mind, they could be in a rush, or they may need more time to build that all-important rapport before revealing more about themselves. It's also possible that they don't have enough knowledge on the topic to delve deeper.

During your small talk, look for signs that they are interested in talking about a topic in more detail. Do their eyes light up? Do they talk faster and with a higher pitch? Are they asking you follow-up questions?

If the answer is no, it might be best to change the subject and continue to look for signs that they want to take the conversation further. Don't take offense or feel like you have failed. There has to be a mutual interest in diving deeper.

Another thing to consider before we jump into the techniques is "netiquette!" Researching people you are about to meet gives you a better idea of their interests, achievements, and even their family and education. If you are meeting a stranger, especially someone you are hoping to date, it's also a sensible idea to make sure they are who they say they are.

At the same time, googling someone before you meet them can come across as a little weird. Some feel that you shouldn't google someone because it will prevent you from asking important questions to get to know a person better, as you may have already discovered the answers.

Generally speaking, googling someone is normally an accepted practice, but there is no universal yes or no as to whether you should. If you don't want to come across as a stalker, use the information you discover to start conversations but avoid things like "I saw online that you . . ." This could easily give the wrong impression.

So, your small talk is going well. What's next?

• Bring energy to the conversation from the beginning: You can feel someone's energy in a conversation, and this reflects their level of interest. While you don't have to be bouncing off the wall, you need to bring the right energy with you.

• Start by inviting others to talk about their feelings: When you discover that someone has moved house or changed jobs, you can ask them what caused the change, giving them a chance to talk about their feelings about a situation without putting too much pressure on them.

• Consider the four main factors of meaningful conversation: It's not the topic of conversation that makes it meaningful. It takes humility, curiosity, generosity, and accountability.

• Ask questions that give people an opportunity to express themselves: Questions like "What was that like?" or "How did that make you feel?" A genuine interest can help the other person feel comfortable opening up.

• Focus on the 'Why' questions, excluding why: When we ask why questions in more meaningful conversations, our tone can take over. We might come across as judging or not understanding why they would do what they did. Try rephrasing why questions.

• Stay motivated: When you feel yourself lacking the motivation to ask questions and actively listen, remember that what you are doing is an act of kindness, and after the conversation, you will have made a difference in that person's life.

• Think of the flow and context: Is this the right atmosphere to have a meaningful conversation? Are there too many people or distractions around? If you are going to be interrupted, the flow will be broken.

• Share more about your feelings: Create links between the topic and how this has impacted your life, relationship, etc. What did you learn from this, and how will it impact your future?

• Be prepared to learn: Learning new things is inspiring. Try to learn something new about the other person, yourself, or a new concept or idea.

• Avoid meaningful conversations with narcissistic people: Anyone who is too concerned about themselves will not be interested in listening to you or showing you any empathy. Just because you listen to them doesn't mean they will listen to you.

Here are some questions that can pave the way for deeper conversations:

• What trait do you still want to have when you are ninety?

• What is your most important goal at the moment?

• What is the one fear you really want to overcome?

• What is something dangerous you have tried?

• If you could have dinner with anyone, dead or alive, who would it be?

• What is your earliest memory?

- What is the biggest trigger of your stress?

- What makes you feel alive?

- What recurring dream or nightmare do you have?

Never feel the urge to force a meaningful conversation. Small talk is perfect for everyone. Deep conversations don't have to occur with everyone we meet. When you start forcing these heavier topics on people, there is a risk that someone could get hurt, normally because they are uncomfortable divulging certain information about themselves. Trust your instincts and the social cues you have learned.

However, the ability to have more meaningful conversations is increased when you meet like-minded people.

How to Meet Like-Minded People

The first thing to do is to get to know those around you better. It sounds ridiculously simple, but there are probably people who you bump into on a regular basis but have only ever touched on the small talk.

If you feel you don't have people around you that you want to connect with, start going to meetups, clubs, and events where there will be people who share your interests. This doesn't include bars, clubs, and parties. These are great places to meet people but not to create that special connection.

This is a good time to reassess your hobbies and interests and then find local activities in the community. Think outside the box, join a hiking club, volunteer at a shelter, or take a computer programming or cookery course. To really step outside the box, start your own online group based on your interest. You don't need to be the expert to bring others together.

As well as hobbies, I like to keep an eye on local community boards (physical and digital) to see if any projects interest me. For example, not long ago, there was a project to start a community plot to grow food for those in need. There is now a group of around twenty-five people who meet up to take care of the plot and also meet for drinks and look for other projects together.

You can also use apps to meet new people. I'm sure you are more than aware of dating apps such as Tinder, but apps like Bumble BFF facilitate platonic relationships. Be selective about the friends you make. It's not about the number of people you meet; it's about taking the time to forge meaningful connections.

When people suggest plans, you might be tempted to say no because you already have so much going on. Your no might just be a front for not breaking out of your comfort zone. Make an effort to say yes to 50 to 70 percent of your invitations.

Finally, and again, ridiculously simple, follow up with those people that you really hit it off with. For some strange reason, you may decide to wait for the next time you accidentally bump into them. But this may only undo some of the work that got you to this point. Do you really want to start over with the small talk and get to know each other again?

Following up with people is how casual relationships turn into lifelong friendships, something we all need!

Why You Want Friends in Adulthood

It's not easy making friends as an adult. We are busy with work, we find a romantic partner, we start a family, and commitments and responsibilities take over our social connections. On top of that, as we grow up and change, it is common to grow apart from the childhood friends we had assumed would be around forever.

But friends in adulthood are crucial for our mental and physical well-being. Loneliness comes with negative secondary effects, but according to research, having strong social connections can increase a person's lifespan (Giles et al. 2005). Friendships can boost heart health and relieve stress.

Aside from the tips we saw in the previous sections, let's look at some other ways to make friends and maintain these important relationships.

• Develop a growth mindset: In order to make new friends, you need to be open to the idea and believe you are capable of doing so.

• Be open to the idea of new experiences: To go along with your growth mindset, you need to get excited about trying new things. If you try a new hobby or activity with a feeling of dread, it's unlikely you are going to enjoy it.

- Make a list of potential friends: Think about the people you have regular contact with and those you would like to get to know better. Make a plan to start a conversation with them.

- Meet the neighbors: If you are used to just waving and saying hi, start with a little more small talk. Remember, being neighbors, you already have something in common.

- Create personal connections with coworkers: Considering how much time you spend with them, it's a good idea to have some friends at work. Once your confidence improves, you could even organize group events.

- Take advantage of your friends on social networks: There may be connections you have with your friends' friends. You can ask them for introductions or network online using people you might know features.

- Use your child's school: Parent-teacher meetings can be a lot more enjoyable when you have a friend there. Again, meeting the parents of your children's friends is another situation where you already have something in common.

- Don't assume you know what friends are thinking: This is particularly true for introverts and overthinkers. If you start to spend more time assuming you know what they are thinking and dwelling on what went wrong, you won't be in the present.

- Remember your emotions are contagious: Don't feel you need to fake a smile all the time because meaningful connections are based on being yourself—the ups and the downs. That being said, relationships that pass the test of time have an element of happiness and positivity.

Above all, when it comes to friends you can trust completely, it's not about quantity. Just because a person has 500 friends on social media doesn't necessarily mean they have meaningful connections. Focus on a few friends and quality relationships. These are the relationships that will bring love, generosity, and humanity!

CONCLUSION

W hen you look at communication in as much detail as we have, it's easy to feel there are too many elements that are almost impossible to get right at the same time, especially when you consider that so many aspects occur in a matter of seconds—if not less.

To be able to communicate with ease and in the most meaningful you, you have to start with your confidence. Only when you are confident in yourself will you realize that you are capable. Confidence takes time to build, but you can start right now with simple changes like adopting a healthy routine, challenging your negative self-talk, and practicing gratitude.

This will be more of an obstacle for those with anxiety disorders, introversion, or shyness. However, with the techniques to overcome anxiety, you can take control of your mind and body and prevent a fight, flight, or freeze mode. When you start overcoming the symptoms of anxiety in social situations, your confidence will start to flourish.

Don't forget to add some mindfulness exercises to your daily routine to keep you in the present. Guided meditation, mindful walks, and grounding exercises using your senses. This won't just improve your confidence but will also reduce overthinking and boost your overall well-being.

When it comes to body language, many people focus on eye contact, which is obviously important, but we have learned how numerous parts of the body can improve the understanding of a message or confuse it. If I could emphasize three things to focus on in the beginning, it would be the right amount of eye contact, a genuine smile, and having an open posture. The rest of our nonverbal cues can be practiced by observing and mirroring others.

By now, you will also have discovered that small talk plays an essential role and is the first step to having meaningful conversations. It's the chance for you to make a positive first impression and ask the right questions to find your common ground.

Along with your engaging small talk and the ability to read people's nonverbal cues, you now know how to turn small talk into a conversation, and with time, these conversations can become more interesting with humor and stories. Only then will you have the rapport with a person to start getting into conversations that involve feelings and life experiences. Without the prep work, neither of you will feel enough trust to open up on a deeper level.

Of course, none of this will be possible if you aren't actively listening. A balanced conversation requires speaking and listening so that both parties feel respected and valued. To actively listen, get rid of your distractions, don't assume you know what the other person is thinking or feeling, and never interrupt!

Without active listening, you won't be able to take in the message, leading to inappropriate responses. Nothing will kill a conversation or create awkwardness like an inappropriate response.

Throughout the chapters, we have seen dozens of open-ended questions that stick to noncontroversial topics for all types of situations and relationship types, from complete strangers to friends. For now, I would like you to create three lists, each with seven questions. One list will have small talk questions, another list will have starters, and the final list will have questions to take your conversations to the next level.

This starter set of questions will give you the confidence to practice communicating in any situation for at least a week. Keep track of the responses and people's reactions. You may notice that some questions are more effective in different situations, and those that don't get the desired results can be switched for others.

You have had barriers to communication, but whatever they have been, you are now prepared to slowly dismantle them. What used to be a problem and something that caused you discomfort will start becoming more natural and even enjoyable. Let go of the preconceived notions and biases you have formed in your mind. The results will be epic!

Finally, don't forget that effective and meaningful conversation is a two-way street. That means that not all of our interactions will always be successful. This isn't necessarily on you. Everybody has their own demons and preconceptions that prevent them from talking with ease. Focus on what you can change to continuously refine your art of communicating and shine brighter in every social situation.

As I've stated in the book, communication is only the first step—and so far, I've communicated my own experiences and knowledge to you. But conversation is where the real social engagement happens, and without your words and views, this book won't ever be a two-way dialogue.

How can you change that? Simply head over to Amazon and leave your opinions and experiences of becoming better at talking to others. I'd love to hear about your journey, and it will allow me to perfectly tie the ribbon on the meaningful journey we began together from the introduction.

SOME BOOKS YOU MAY FIND INTERESTING

How to Read People Like a Book

Speed-Read, Analyze, and Understand Anyone's Body Language, Emotions, and Thoughts

Stop racking your brain to figure out what others are really trying to say... know how to instantly decode the meaning behind their unspoken messages.

You don't have to be a communication expert, detective, or superhero to learn how to recognize and decode social cues.

All you need to do is to know exactly what to look for and what they really mean.

Fortunately, this book contains everything you need to know about deciphering other people's silent messages.

Inside, here is just a fraction of what you will discover:

• How to interpret facial expressions, body language, tone of voice, and other nonverbal cues – spare yourself from any miscommunication!

- **50+ social cues that will clue you in on what a person is thinking or feeling**... no more guessing games that could lead you to trouble

- What "clusters of gestures" are and why they are crucial to reading other people

- **25+ effective ways to tell if someone's lying — make any seasoned detective proud with your skills**

- Factors that affect how you read people — avoid getting the wrong conclusion about someone!

- **How to read between the lines using verbal cues... their choice of words matters more than you think!**

- Fool-proof ways to identify the tone of a text or email

Every day, you encounter dozens of social cues without knowing how powerful they are or how you can use them to your advantage.

It's time to flip the narrative — by learning how to accurately read other people, you will not just boost your communication skills... you'll foster deeper connections and enjoy improved relationships more than ever.

Master the art of nonverbal communication and read people like a pro.

How to Stop Negative Thinking

The 7-Step Plan to Eliminate Negativity, Overcome Rumination, Cease Overthinking Spiral, and Change Your Toxic Thoughts to Healthy Self-Talk

There is a massive amount of shame that comes with negative thinking. You blame yourself for the intrusive thoughts that blindside you. You feel guilty for not being more optimistic. **It's time to stop.**

Negative thinking isn't as simple as someone looking at the glass half empty. It is a **debilitating mindset** that seeps into every area of your life.

Negative thinking happens automatically – **it's not your fault.**

You tell yourself that today will be a better day, but your brain tells you the opposite, and you slip back into old negative habits.

But that doesn't mean that negative thinking is something you can't control.

The brain is indeed negatively biased. However, science has confirmed that **you can rewire the way you think**.

And you can start doing this today!

In *How to Stop Negative Thinking*, here is just a fraction of what you will discover:

- How to **overcome every type of negative thinking** from intrusive thoughts to rumination in 7 simple steps

- Simple, effective strategies with **practice exercises** that will help you overcome the negative thought patterns that prevent you from leading the life you want

- 3 crucial tools you can use to pinpoint the roots of your negative thinking

- **Scientifically proven breathing techniques** that will ease the impact of negative thoughts and rumination

- How to **put a stop to toxic behavior, passive aggression, and toxic positivity** and protect your new mindset

- **How to love and accept yourself despite your negative thinking** – discover why this is crucial to kickstart your journey towards a happier, more positive person

Just by reading this, you have taken control and decided to change. Now all that's missing is the final step.

If you are ready to take the next step towards a more positive life, then scan the QR code right now.

Healthy Boundaries

How to Set Strong Boundaries, Say No Without Guilt, and Maintain Good Relationships With Your Parents, Family, and Friends

Discover the power of self-love, and learn how to set healthy boundaries – without feeling guilty.

Do you ever wonder what it would be like if the people you care about respected your personal space? Do you wish that there was an easy way to say "No" every time you don't want to say "Yes"?

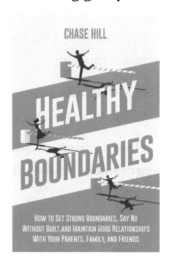

If this is you, then you've probably had moments of trying to please others – often, to your own detriment.

Perhaps you have an inability to say "No" because you don't want to disappoint or anger the other person… leading you to do things you never wanted to do in the first place…

What's worse, when you do try to set up boundaries, people will label you as mean or moody. It will seem impossible to make people respect your decisions without starting conflict.

But there's a simple way to solve your problems!

You can start doing what YOU want to do. You don't have to compromise your individuality just to be "considerate" of others. You can set healthy boundaries, and make your friends, family and parents **respect that boundary.**

In *Healthy Boundaries*, here's just a taste of what you'll discover:

• **A step-by-step guide to setting healthy personal boundaries without starting an argument**

• 5 dangerous mistakes you *must* avoid when setting boundaries

• The secret to saying "No" **without feeling guilty** – and without being misunderstood

• How to stop constantly apologizing, and find out when you should and shouldn't be sorry

• 10 debilitating myths that are stopping you from setting up boundaries – and how to troubleshoot them

• How to detoxify your emotions and release toxicity from your system like a breath of fresh air

• **A clear path** to give you the freedom to love yourself, follow what YOU want, and prioritize yourself

If you're ready to start living the life you deserve without feeling guilty, then scan this QR code right now!

How to Stop Overthinking

The 7-Step Plan to Control and Eliminate Negative Thoughts, Declutter Your Mind and Start Thinking Positively in 5 Minutes or Less

If you want to break free from toxic thoughts, silence your mental chatter, and show your mind who's boss... then keep reading!

Do you find yourself constantly stressed out, imagining worst-case scenarios?

How many times have you replayed previous conversations in your head, wishing you'd handled them better?

Are you tired of missing out on fun and exciting things in life because you tend to analyze decisions over and over again?

If these situations sound relatable, you may be part of the 73% of adults who suffer from overthinking.

Overthinking may be a hard habit to break, but it's completely doable... with the right guide and support.

This book is designed to be your simple roadmap, to help you navigate the treacherous path of overthinking and ultimately escape these unhealthy habits for good!

Inside, here is just a small fraction of what you will discover:

- **60+ fool-proof techniques** to stop overthinking, overcome fears, and remove toxic thoughts from your mind

- A simple quiz to find out if you are an over-thinker and to what degree… so you'll know the best ways to address it

- **Quick and easy steps to relax your brain when it's on overdrive** – be calm and carry on in no time

- What "ruminating" is and why you should quit doing it at all costs

- **9 signs that you are stuck in a vicious cycle of overthinking**

- **Secrets to quiet your mind and find inner peace** – discover how to finally get that negative voice out of your head

- **How to handle toxic people in your life** – stop them from sucking your positive energy and the fun in life

With practice, and proper guidance, you can break free from overthinking and finally start living the life you've been dreaming of.

Kick overthinking to the curb once and for all… scan this QR code right now.

A FREE GIFT TO OUR READERS

I'd like to give you a gift as a way of saying thanks for your purchase!

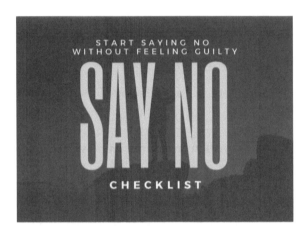

This checklist includes:

- 8 steps to start saying no.
- 12 must-dos to stop feeling guilty.
- 9 healthy ways to say no.

The last thing we want is for your mood to be ruined because you weren't prepared.

To receive your Say No Checklist, visit the link:

www.chasehillbooks.com

Prefer a quick access? Scan the QR code below:

If you have any difficulty downloading the checklist, contact me at **chase@chasehillbooks.com,** and I'll send you a copy as soon as possible.

RESOURCES

4 steps to change your words, change your life | Tony Robbins. (2022, April 29). tonyrobbins.com. https://www.tonyrobbins.com/mind-meaning/change-your-words-change-your-life/

23 Tips to Be Confident in a Conversation (With Examples). (2022, February 3). SocialSelf. https://socialself.com/confident-conversation/

A Guide to Productively Communicating Your Feelings. (2022, March 16). Psych Company. https://www.psychcompany.com/2019/productively-communicating-your-feelings/

Are You Too Quiet? Understanding Shyness. (n.d.). https://www.betterup.com/blog/what-is-shyness

Barnard, D. (2018, January 20). *Average speaking rate and words per minute.* Virtual Speech. https://virtualspeech.com/blog/average-speaking-rate-words-per-minute

Berkman, L. F., & Syme, S. L. (1979, February). *Social networks, host resistance, and mortality: A nine-year follow-up study of Alameda County residents.* National Library of Medicine. https://pubmed.ncbi.nlm.nih.gov/425958/

Clear, J. (2018, July 26). *Body Language Hacks: Be Confident and Reduce Stress in 2 Minutes*. James Clear. https://jamesclear.com/body-language-how-to-be-confident

Colin, C., & Baedeker, R. (2022, October 16). *How to turn small talk into smart conversation*. ideas.ted.com. https://ideas.ted.com/how-to-turn-small-talk-into-smart-conversation/

Davis, K. (1947, March). *Final note on a case of extreme isolation*. JSTOR. https://www.jstor.org/stable/2770825

Edwards, V. van. (2021, October 25). *Learn the 5 Levels of Social Cues with Jordan Harbinger*. Science of People. https://www.scienceofpeople.com/social-cues/

Edwards, V. van. (2022, January 19). *The Ultimate Guide To Making a Great First Impression (even online)*. Science of People. https://www.scienceofpeople.com/first-impressions/

Giles, L. C., Glonek, G. F. V., Luszcz, M. A., & Andrews, G. R. (2005, July 1). *Effect of social networks on 10 year survival in very old Australians: the Australian longitudinal study of aging*. Journal of Epidemiology & Community Health. https://jech.bmj.com/content/59/7/574.full

Gurteen, D. (n.d.). *Listen with the intent to understand*. Conversational Leadership. https://conversational-leadership.net/listen-to-understand/

Hariri-Kia, I. (2020, September 5). *Your Holiday Guide to Small Talk, According to 3 People Who Do It for a Living*. Repeller. https://repeller.com/small-talk-tips/

How to Carry a Conversation — the Art of Making Connections. (n.d.). https://www.betterup.com/blog/how-to-carry-a-conversation

How to Have Deeper and More Meaningful Conversations. (2022, January 6). Medium. https://medium.com/@joshfelber/how-to-have-deeper-and-more-meaningful-conversations-f1d254bf066e

How to Start a Conversation. (2022, November 22). Verywell Mind. https://www.verywellmind.com/how-to-start-a-conversation-4582339

Inside Higher Ed. (2016, May 18). *How to keep emotions from leading your communications (essay).* https://www.insidehighered.com/advice/2016/05/18/how-keep-emotions-leading-your-communications-essay

Kelly, A. (2017, October 3). *The psychology of first impressions.* Imagine Health. https://imaginehealth.ie/psychology-first-impressions/

Kishore, K. (2021, August 13). *Why Are Social Skills Important?* Harappa. https://harappa.education/harappa-diaries/meaning-and-importance-+of-social-skills/

Make Deep & Meaningful Conversations. (2021, December 7). Get the Friends You Want. https://getthefriendsyouwant.com/make-deep-meaningful-conversations/

Miller, K. (2021, November 18). *12 Tips for How To End a Conversation Instead of Dying a Thousand Deaths in Moments of Awkward Silence.* Well+Good. https://www.wellandgood.com/how-to-end-conversation/

MindTools | Home. (n.d.). https://www.mindtools.-com/az4wxv7/active-listening

NHS website. (2022, March 29). *Social anxiety (social phobia).* nhs.uk. https://www.nhs.uk/mental-health/conditions/social-anxiety/

O'Bryan, A., PhD. (2022, November 18). *How to Practice Active Listening: 16 Examples & Techniques.* PositivePsychology.com. https://positivepsychology.com/active-listening-techniques/

Roberts, D. (2019, December 30). *Why small talk is so excruciating.* Vox. https://www.vox.-com/2015/7/7/8903123/small-talk

Sandstrom, G., & Dunn, E. (2014, May). *Is efficiency overrated.* Researchgate. https://www.researchgate.net/publication/278098105_Is_-Efficiency_Overrated

Shi, M. (2020, April 17). *Associations of emotional intelligence and gratitude with empathy in medical students - BMC Medical Education.* BioMed Central.https://bmcmededuc.biomed-central.com/articles/10.1186/s12909-020-02041-4

Siggins, K. (2022, October 16). *How To Be More Confident When Talking To People.* Everyday Power. https://everyday-power.com/be-more-confident-talking-to-people/

Steiger, N. (2019, October 15). *"The single biggest problem in communication is the illusion that it has taken place." George Bernard Shaw.* Nancy Steiger. https://www.nancysteigerconsulting.-com/thinking-out-loud-1/2019/10/15/the-single-biggest-problem-in-communication-is-the-illusion-that-it-has-taken-place-george-bernard-shaw

The Scientific World. (2020, December 27). *The Importance of Communication Skills in Everyday Life*. The Scientific World - Let's Have a Moment of Science. https://www.scientific-worldinfo.com/2020/12/importance-of-communication-skills-in-everyay-life.html

Small Talk Topics. (2022, February 14). Verywell Mind. https://www.verywellmind.com/small-talk-topics-3024421

Some Thoughts On The Point Of Small Talk | www.succeedsocially.com. (n.d.). https://www.succeed-socially.com/smalltalk

Specktor, B. (2021, July 26). *9 Magic Phrases That Can Save Awkward Conversations*. Reader's Digest. https://www.rd.com/list/conversation-skills/

The Balanced Conversation Cycle. (n.d.). Revolution Learning and Development Ltd. https://www.revolutionlearning.co.uk/article/the-balanced-conversation-cycle/

Thompson, J. (2011, September 30). *Is non-verbal communication a numbers game?* Psychology Today. https://www.psychologytoday.com/us/blog/beyond-words/201109/is-nonverbal-communication-numbers-game

Types of Nonverbal Communication. (2022, October 12). Verywell Mind. https://www.verywellmind.com/types-of-nonverbal-communication-2795397

Made in United States
Troutdale, OR
11/16/2024